The Trial of Charles Manson
California Cult Murders

by Bradley Steffens
and Craig L. Staples

FAMOUS
TRIALS

LUCENT BOOKS
SAN DIEGO, CALIFORNIA

THOMSON

GALE

*Detroit • New York • San Diego • San Francisco
Boston • New Haven, Conn. • Waterville, Maine
London • Munich*

Titles in the Famous Trials series include:

The Boston Massacre
Cherokee Nation v. Georgia
The Dred Scott Decision
Engle v. Vitale
Furman v. Georgia
The Impeachment of Bill
  Clinton
Miranda v. Arizona
The Nuremberg Trials
The O.J. Simpson Trial

The Pentagon Papers
Roe v. Wade
The Rosenberg Espionage
  Case
The Salem Witch Trials
The Scopes Trial
The Trial of Adolf Eichmann
The Trial of Joan of Arc
The Trial of John Brown
The Trial of Socrates

To Jeanette

Library of Congress Cataloging-in-Publication Data

Steffens, Bradley
  The Trial of Charles Manson: California cult murders / by Bradley
Steffens and Craig L. Staples.
    p. cm. — (Famous trials)
Includes bibliographical references and index.
Summary: Explores the 1969 murders of actress Sharon Tate
and others by members of the "Manson Family," the subsequent
investigation and trials, and the strange hold Charles Manson
continues to have over people.
  ISBN 1-56006-733-0 (hc : alk. paper)
  1. Manson, Charles, 1934– —Trials, litigation, etc.—Juvenile
literature. 2. Trials (Murder)—California—Junvenile literature.
3. Mass murder—California—Juvenile literature. [1. Manson,
Charlers, 1934– —Trials, litigation, etc. 2. Trials (Murder) 3. Mass
murder.] I. Title. II. Series.
  KF224.M212 S73 2002
  345.73'02523—dc21

2001004396

Table of Contents

Foreword

"The law is not an end in and of itself, nor does it provide ends. It is preeminently a means to serve what we think is right."

William J. Brennan Jr.

THE CONCEPT OF JUSTICE AND THE RULE OF LAW are hallmarks of Western civilization, manifested perhaps most visibly in widely famous and dramatic court trials. These trials include such important and memorable personages as the ancient Greek philosopher Socrates, who was accused and convicted of corrupting the minds of his society's youth in 399 B.C.; the French maiden and military leader Joan of Arc, accused and convicted of heresy against the church in 1431; to former football star O.J. Simpson, acquitted of double murder in 1995. These and other well-known and controversial trials constitute the most public, and therefore most familiar, demonstrations of a Western legal tradition that dates back through the ages. Although no one is certain when the first law code appeared or when the first formal court trials were held, Babylonian ruler Hammurabi introduced the first known law code in about 1760 B.C. It remains unclear how this code was administered, and no records of specific trials have survived. What is clear, however, is that humans have always sought to govern behavior and define actions in terms of law.

Almost all societies have made laws and prosecuted people for going against those laws, but the question of which behaviors to sanction and which to censure has always been controversial and remains in flux. Some, such as Roman orator and legislator Cicero, argue that laws are simply applications of universal standards. Cicero believed that humanity would agree on what constituted illegal behavior and that human laws were a mere extension of natural laws. "True law is right reason in agreement with nature," he wrote,

4

world-wide in scope, unchanging, everlasting. . . . We may not oppose or alter that law, we cannot abolish it, we cannot be freed from its obligations by any legislature. . . .This [natural] law does not differ for Rome and for Athens, for the present and for the future. . . . It is and will be valid for all nations and all times.

Cicero's rather optimistic view has been contradicted throughout history, however. For every law made to preserve harmony and set universal standards of behavior, another has been born of fear, prejudice, greed, desire for power, and a host of other motives. History is replete with individuals defying and fighting to change such laws—and even to topple governments that dictate such laws. Abolitionists fought against slavery, civil rights leaders fought for equal rights, millions throughout the world have fought for independence—these constitute a minimum of reasons for which people have sought to overturn laws that they believed to be wrong or unjust. In opposition to Cicero, then, many others, such as eighteenth-century English poet and philosopher William Godwin, believe humans must be constantly vigilant against bad laws. As Godwin said in 1793:

> Laws we sometimes call the wisdom of our ancestors. But this is a strange imposition. It was as frequently the dictate of their passion, of timidity, jealousy, a monopolizing spirit, and a lust of power that knew no bounds. Are we not obliged perpetually to renew and remodel this misnamed wisdom of our ancestors? To correct it by a detection of their ignorance, and a censure of their intolerance?

Lucent Books' *Famous Trials* series showcases trials that exemplify both society's praiseworthy condemnation of universally unacceptable behavior, and its misguided persecution of individuals based on fear and ignorance, as well as trials that leave open the question of whether justice has been done. Each volume begins by setting the scene and providing a historical context to show how society's mores influence the trial process and the verdict.

Each book goes on to present a detailed and lively account of the trial, including liberal use of primary source material such as direct testimony, lawyers' summations, and contemporary and modern commentary. In addition, sidebars throughout the text create a broader context by presenting illuminating details about important points of law, information on key personalities, and important distinctions related to civil, federal, and criminal procedures. Thus, all of the primary and secondary source material included in both the text and the sidebars demonstrates to readers the sources and methods historians use to derive information and conclusions about such events.

Lastly, each *Famous Trials* volume includes one or more of the following comprehensive tools that motivate readers to pursue further reading and research. A timeline allows readers to see the scope of the trial at a glance, annotated bibliographies provide both sources for further research and a thorough list of works consulted, a glossary helps students with unfamiliar words and concepts, and a comprehensive index permits quick scanning of the book as a whole.

The insight of Oliver Wendell Holmes Jr., distinguished Supreme Court justice, exemplifies the theme of the *Famous Trials* series. Taken from *The Common Law*, published in 1881, Holmes remarked: "The life of the law has not been logic, it has been experience." That "experience" consists mainly in how laws are applied in society and challenged in the courts, a process resulting in differing outcomes from one generation to the next. Thus, the *Famous Trials* series encourages readers to examine trials within a broader historical and social context.

Introduction

The Killer Cult

THE BRUTAL SLAYINGS of actress Sharon Tate and four others at her Hollywood home on August 9, 1969, and the murders the following night of businessman Leno LaBianca and his wife, Rosemary, terrified Southern Californians and shocked all of America. The subsequent arrest and trial of Charles Manson, a thirty-four-year-old former convict and self-styled guru, along with several members of his cult following, ultimately revealed the unexpected and chilling motives behind seven homicides that stand alone in the history of American crime for savagery and sheer strangeness.

"No Name Maddox"

Ironically, the man whose name would become one of the most infamous in the history of crime started life with no name at all. Charles Manson's birth certificate, issued on November 12, 1934, reads "no name Maddox—a boy."

Born to an unmarried sixteen-year-old girl named Kathleen Maddox and an itinerant worker known only as Colonel Scott, the child received the name Manson when his mother married William Manson. From the start, Charles Manson's family life was unstable. His mother divorced Manson and moved about constantly, sometimes with Charles, sometimes without him. When the boy was five, his mother was imprisoned for burglary, and Charles was left with relatives. Manson's mother eventually abandoned her responsibilities entirely, leaving her son in the care of a succession of boys' homes.

At age fourteen Charles was accepted into Boys Town, the acclaimed orphanage in Nebraska. The teenage Charles stayed for four days before he and another boy stole a car and lived for a time on the road, stealing to get money. When Charles was apprehended, he was sent to a reform school, the Indiana School for Boys. By the time he was sixteen, Charles's life was well on its way to becoming what the *New York Times Magazine* would later call "a monument to parental neglect and the failure of the public correctional system."[1] A list of his criminal convictions soon ran to a half-dozen typed pages and included auto theft, breaking and entering, burglary, and armed robbery. Every parole granted to Charles Manson ended in failure.

At age thirty-two, Manson had spent more than half of his life in some kind of correctional facility. He had become, according to a prison counselor's report, "an almost classic textbook case of the correctional institutional inmate,"[2] so much so that at the end of a ten-year sentence in 1967, Manson begged his guards to let him stay in prison. His request was denied. On March 21, 1967, Manson was taken to Los Angeles and was released. The words of an earlier prison report would prove prophetic: "This inmate will no doubt be in serious difficulty soon."[3]

Charles Manson, the man who began life with no name, delights in changing his appearance.

The America that greeted Manson when he emerged from prison in 1967 was vastly different from the one he had left in 1959. The sixties had brought a period of unrest unlike any the country had seen since the Civil War. Black and white Americans had been fighting for most of the decade over issues of racial discrimination and civil rights. The fight for social equality had fostered peaceful protest marches and demonstrations, but it had also caused devastating outbreaks of rioting, looting, and destruction in the African American neighborhoods of some of America's largest cities.

The New Generation

The civil rights dispute was not the only issue troubling the nation during the sixties. For the first time in memory, the country was fighting a foreign war that did not have popular support. Most vocal in their disapproval of the war in Vietnam were the young Americans who were reaching college age during the sixties —the baby boom generation, nicknamed for the boom in the birth rate in America at the close of World War II. Vast numbers of baby boomers questioned virtually every value espoused by the generations that had come before them.

Opposition to America's involvement in the Vietnam War and to the nation's policy of forced military service—known as the draft—became a rallying point for millions of disenchanted young Americans. A campaign of protest and dissent spread across the college campuses and public forums of America. Sympathies for and against the issues raised by the war and by the civil rights movement seemed to fall along lines of age, and social commentators began to speak of America's so-called generation gap.

The philosophies that divided the sides of the generation gap went beyond politics. Many young Americans were dissatisfied with the conventional lifestyle of their parents and were searching for an alternative way of life to take its place. The baby boom generation was the most prosperous and well-educated generation in American history, but, paradoxically, that prosperity contributed to a sense of restlessness and discontent. Many baby boomers rejected crass materialism and embraced a lifestyle endorsed by a counterculture movement whose members called themselves hippies.

Hippies disdained the orthodox work ethic and family living groups that defined America's middle class throughout most of the 1900s. Hippies called themselves flower children and flaunted their group identity with colorful costume and dress; the men adopted unconventionally long hairstyles. Almost all hippies enjoyed the guitar-based rock music of groups such as the Beatles, the Rolling Stones, Jefferson Airplane, the Grateful Dead, the Doors, and others. Many in the hippie culture promoted the use of mind-altering drugs as a recreational or spiritual outlet. With its allure of personal freedom, the carefree hippie life enticed many of those who were coming of age during the sixties. The breakdown of traditional social conventions had a downside, however. Some hippies drifted into an unstructured and unstable existence.

The Gardener and His Flower Children

Within this social context, Charles Manson began to gather the misfits and runaways that became the Manson Family. Just five feet, two inches tall and youthful in appearance, Manson tended to fit in with the younger crowd he found in the Haight-Ashbury section of San Francisco and on college campuses where he often played his guitar and hung out. One of Manson's first recruits, eighteen-year-old Lynette Fromme, was typical of the Family members. Fromme, who would become known by the nickname "Squeaky," had grown up in middle-class Westchester, California. Fromme had excelled in drama and literature at Redondo Beach High School, but her teenage years left her unsatisfied and unfulfilled. To Fromme, middle-class life was a sham that hid vast emotional barrenness.

After being ordered out of the family home by her father in 1967, Fromme met Manson at a public beach where she had been spending her days. Accompanied by a young woman named Mary Brunner, Manson was drifting between Los Angeles and San Francisco trying to establish himself as a musician. Manson convinced Fromme to join him and Brunner on their

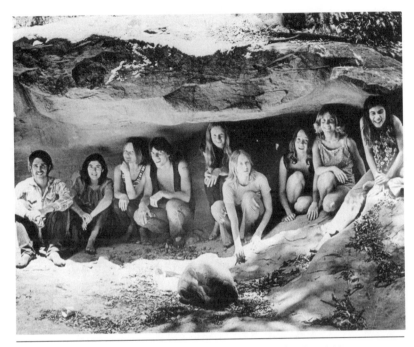

The core of the Manson Family poses for a photographer in 1968.

carefree adventure. Up and down the California coast, Manson told the impressionable young teenagers that he was a "gardener" traveling the country to tend to his "flower children." Shortly after Fromme joined up with Manson, Patricia Krenwinkel, another unhappy baby boomer, quit her job and joined the group. The Manson "Family" was born.

Over the next year scores of aimless or curious hippies joined the group on its travels. Most eventually left, but some—such as Bobby Beausoleil, Leslie Van Houten, Charles "Tex" Watson, and Susan Atkins—remained. By October 1968 Manson had formed the core of his Family. This group of a dozen or so followers was fiercely loyal to Charles Manson. Soon there was nothing they refused to do for him—even kill.

Manson preached of an impending violent social revolution that would bring an end to the established order in America. The doomsday doctrine, which Manson concocted from pieces of biblical scripture, snatches of popular song lyrics, and tenets borrowed from the Church of Scientology, was known to the members of the Manson Family as Helter Skelter. Manson envisioned himself emerging as the leader of the new social order that would arise from the ashes of revolution. The campaign of terror that Manson ordered in August 1969 was to be the start of Helter Skelter.

The trial of the Manson Family in what became known as the Tate-LaBianca murders was the longest and costliest murder trial in American history. It highlighted the growing rift between two generations of Americans and cast an ominous pall over the carefree hippie lifestyle. The trial was a media event that spawned a seemingly endless fascination in Americans with the counter-culture, the occult, and the world of illegal and mind-altering drugs. It established the word *cult* in the everyday conversation of America. Most of all, the trial inscribed the name of Charles Manson into the annals of criminal history as one of the most dia-bolical masterminds of all time.

Chapter 1

Horror in Hollywood

"**N**OTHING BUT BODIES."[4] POLICE radios carried this message to Los Angeles Police Department (LAPD) headquarters early on the morning of August 9, 1969. The LAPD officers had responded to the emergency call of a maid who worked at 10050 Cielo Drive in an exclusive neighborhood of Bel Air, California. What the responding officers had found was one of the bloodiest crime scenes in American history. It was also one of the most baffling. Weapons, fingerprints, and a reasonable motive all were missing. For four long months, while the public worried about who the killers were and who their next victims might be, the investigation led nowhere. Only through a police officer's hunch and a clue that came from more than two hundred miles away did authorities learn who was behind the crime and what the motives for the killings actually were.

Sharon Tate and her husband, Roman Polanski, were one of the most glamorous couples in Hollywood.

A Gruesome Scene

The house on Cielo Drive was the residence of actress Sharon Tate and her husband, Roman Polanski. Polanski was a successful and controversial movie director, whose horror film *Rosemary's*

Baby had been a worldwide hit the previous summer. Tate was a beautiful starlet who had starred in *Valley of the Dolls*, *Fearless Vampire Killers*, and other movies.

What police found at the Polanski home that summer morning was more gruesome than anything American moviegoers had ever witnessed. In the driveway of the sprawling home, a young man's lifeless body lay behind the steering wheel of his car. He had been shot four times in the head. Across the lawn lay the dead body of a dark-haired woman dressed only in a nightgown. She had been stabbed twenty-nine times. Near her was the battered body of a man. He had been stabbed fifty-one times and had been beaten so savagely that the officers were barely able to make out his facial features.

Inside the home the carnage was even worse. A young, pregnant woman had been knifed to death. She was lying in a pool of blood, her unborn child lifeless in her womb. The rope tied around her legs and hands led policemen to yet another body.

The Los Angeles Police Department investigates the grisly murder scene.

MARRIED IN A MINISKIRT

Actress Sharon Tate bears the tragic distinction of being one of the most beautiful and glamorous murder victims in the history of American crime. Tate won her first beauty pageant, Miss Tiny Tot, at the age of seven months. It was to be the first of a dozen beauty titles she would win.

When she was eighteen, Tate had a chance meeting with actor Richard Beymer. This encounter led to an interview with television producer Martin Ransohoff. Impressed with Tate's beauty and poise, Ransohoff signed the aspiring actress to an exclusive contract the next day.

Ransohoff gave Tate minor roles in his television series *The Beverly Hillbillies* and *Mr. Ed*. She went on to star in several small films before she met Roman Polanski, a young jet-set movie director. Their 1968 wedding in London's Playboy Club was a celebrity event. The bride was the pinnacle of fashion: For a wedding gown, she wore a white designer miniskirt.

Tate retired from acting when she learned she was pregnant, telling friends and associates that she was going to focus on her family. She filled her house with everything a baby would need. Two weeks before her delivery date, she was murdered by the Manson Family. Her unborn child was wrapped in a shroud and was placed next to her in the coffin. Tate was dressed in her favorite blue and yellow miniskirt.

Sharon Tate remains an icon of 1960s popular culture. In his book *Sharon Tate and the Manson Murders*, Greg King voices the regret many feel that Tate's memory is forever linked to Charles Manson.

Actress Sharon Tate.

To many, Sharon Tate remains a minor character in an American saga of mass carnage, counter-culture, and insanity, a cast member whose glittering orbit encompassed the elite of Hollywood's movie and music worlds, but whose beautiful surface cloaked a darker reality. To her family and friends, however, Sharon Tate remains an unforgettable presence, a vibrant ghost whose beauty, gentle spirit, and love cannot be erased by the passage of time.

Sharon Tate's body is removed from the house, which had become a scene of brutal carnage.

The fashionably dressed young man lying near her had been shot in the chest and had been stabbed repeatedly. He was lying face down in his own blood, his head covered with a bloody towel.

The Polanskis' maid, Winifred Chapman, identified the pregnant woman as Sharon Tate. Chapman informed the officers that Roman Polanski was overseas making a movie. The officers summoned Polanski's business manager, William Tennant, to the crime scene to help identify the dead. As soon as Tennant arrived at the house, authorities escorted him across police barricades.

Tennant did not recognize the teenager who had been murdered in the driveway, but he confirmed that the woman in the house was twenty-six-year-old Tate. He identified the three other victims: The woman on the front lawn was Abigail "Gibby" Folger, a twenty-five-year-old philanthropist and heiress to the Folger Coffee fortune. The man near Folger was her boyfriend, Wojiciech "Voytek" Frykowski, a friend of Polanski since their days together in their native Poland. Folger and Frykowski had been staying as guests in the Polanski home. Inside the home, alongside Tate, was thirty-five-year-old Jay Sebring, a wealthy entrepreneur who had pioneered the concept of men's hair-styling in America, turning it into a multimillion-dollar business. Sebring was also a family friend of the Polanskis. At one time he had even been Tate's fiancé. The dead teenage boy lay in the morgue as "John Doe" for hours until police identified him as eighteen-year-old Steven Parent, who had recently graduated from high school and was working at an electronics store.

Media Frenzy

Minutes after law enforcement officials arrived at the scene of the crime, reporters and cameramen began gathering outside the gates of the Polanski home. Members of the press, who had been tipped off by the dispatches on police radios, sensed a good story, but investigators were not offering details about the crime. Word leaked out that Tate and the others were the victims of a ritual slaying. Whole articles were thrown together based solely on rumor and speculation. The media frenzy that began that day would continue for months and even come to play a part in the trial.

While the reporters outside the grounds pressed every visitor to the crime scene for tidbits of information, the investigators inside the compound combed the area for clues. What they found was yet another twist in the bizarre case. While patrolling the grounds, officers were drawn to the rear of the property by the sound of a barking dog. As they neared a small guest house at the back of the property, they heard a voice telling the dog to be quiet. The officers burst into the guest house with guns drawn and subdued the startled young man inside. He was arrested, handcuffed, and taken to police headquarters. The LAPD quickly called a press conference to announce that William Garretson, the nineteen-year-old property groundskeeper they had apprehended at the scene of the crime, was the prime suspect in the murders of Tate and her house guests.

Garretson denied having any part in the crime. He even agreed to take a lie-detector test to establish his innocence. Before

The murders are front page news in the Los Angeles Times.

police had a chance to administer the test to Garretson, bloody events unfolding in the early hours of Sunday morning cast doubt on his involvement in the killings.

A Second Night of Murders

Sometime between the hours of two and three on Sunday morning, August 10, 1969, a prominent businessman and his wife were murdered in their home in an upscale neighborhood of Los Angeles. The scene that greeted officers at the

'RITUALISTIC SLAYINGS'

Sharon Tate, Four Others Murdered

BY DIAL TORGERSON
Times Staff Writer

Sharon Tate
Times photo

Film star Sharon Tate, another woman and three men were found slain Saturday, their bodies scattered around a Benedict Canyon estate in what police said resembled a ritualistic mass murder.

The victims were shot, stabbed or throttled. On the front door of the home, written in blood, was one word: "Pig."

Police arrested the only one left alive on the property—a 19-year-old houseboy. He was booked on suspicion of murder.

Killed were:

—Miss Tate, 26, a star of "Valley of the Dolls" and wife of Roman Polanski, director of "Rosemary's

Related story, pictures on Page B.

Baby." She was eight months pregnant. He is in England.

—Abigail Folger, 26, heiress to the Folger's Coffee family.

—Jay Sebring, 35, once Miss Tate's fiance, a Hollywood hair stylist credited with launching the trend to hair styling for men.

— Voityck Frokowski, 37, who worked with Polanski in Polish films before they came to Hollywood.

—Steven Parent, 18, of El Monte, who left his home Friday morning after telling his family he was going to "go to Beverly Hills."

A maid, Mrs. Winifred Chapman, went to the sprawling home at the end of Cielo Drive at 8:30 a.m. to begin her day's work. What she found sent her running to a neighbor's home in a state of shock:

In a white two-door sedan in the driveway was the body of the young man, slumped back in the driver's seat, shot to death.

On the lawn in front of the ranch-style home was the body of Frokowski.

Twenty yards away, under a fir tree on the well-trimmed lawn, was the body of Miss Folger, clad in a nightgown.

In the living room, dressed in underwear—bikini panties and a brassiere—was Miss Tate. A bloodied nylon cord was around her neck. It ran over a beam in the open-beam ceiling and was tied around the neck of Sebring, whose body lay nearby. Over Sebring's head was a black

Please Turn to Page 18, Col. 1

home of Leno and Rosemary LaBianca was as grisly as the one at the Polanskis' home the previous night. The LaBiancas had been beaten and stabbed. A knife was lodged in Leno LaBianca's throat, and a carving fork was impaled in his stomach. The word *war* had been carved into his flesh. Blood had been smeared on the walls of the kitchen and living room.

The news of a second set of murders left Los Angeles gripped in terror. "Second Ritual Killings Here" read one newspaper headline on Monday morning. "Link to 5-Way Murder Seen!"[5] read the subhead. Southern California's celebrities and movie stars went into hiding; some even made plans to move from the area. John Phillips, a member of the popular rock group the Mamas and the Papas and a neighbor of the Polanskis, later recalled what the panic was like:

In the aftermath of the Tate murders, paranoia swept through Beverly Hills and Bel Air. Rumors of a "hit list" began to spread. . . . There were bizarre theories that attempted to link the murders to LSD and Satanic rites, kinky and deadly sexual perversions, and, somehow, to Polanski's own penchant for violence in movies. You had to wait in line at sporting goods stores to buy guns. I immediately went out that Saturday and bought a nine-millimeter Browning (a powerful handgun). . . . I concealed knives all over the house. It was a great time to be in the attack dog, bodyguard, electronic alarm, or armed security business. The demand for security guards was so great that I think the security firms were hiring Eagle Scouts. . . . Everyone was terrified, waiting to see who would be sacrificed next. No one felt safe. We were afraid to fall asleep.[6]

Meanwhile the LAPD tried to calm fears that a serial killer was on the loose. Inspector K.J. McCauley discounted the idea that the same killer was responsible for the LaBianca and the Tate murders. "I don't see any connection between this murder and the others," McCauley told reporters. "They're too widely removed. I just don't see any connection." One possibility, the LAPD suggested, was that the LaBianca murders were the work of a copycat killer, a second murderer who mimics the circumstances of a well-known crime. "There is a similarity," Sergeant Bryce Houchin admitted, "but whether it's the same suspect or a copycat we just don't know."[7]

Growing Doubt

Like many people in Southern California and across America, Paul Whiteley and Charles Guenther doubted the LAPD's copycat killer theory. Unlike the average citizens who followed the story on television and in the newspapers, however, Whiteley and Guenther based their conclusion on professional information. Homicide detectives with the Los Angeles County Sheriff's Office, Whiteley and Guenther had investigated a murder that seemed very similar to the Tate-LaBianca murders but had occurred at the end of July. Since details about this murder were not known outside Whiteley and Guenther's office, it seemed unlikely that its similarity to the Tate-LaBianca slayings could be attributed to the work of a copycat killer.

On July 31 the Los Angeles County Sheriff's Office had received a call from a friend of Gary Hinman, a music teacher who lived in Topanga Canyon near the town of Santa Monica, California. The caller said that Hinman had not been seen for days, his mailbox was overflowing, and repeated phone calls to his house had gone unanswered. Officers drove out to Hinman's remote cabin and, after knocking, let themselves in. Inside the hot cabin they discovered Hinman's rotting corpse. The victim had been stabbed and left to die. Nothing of value had been taken from inside the home, but Hinman's two automobiles were missing from the driveway.

A Bloody Clue

As details of Sharon Tate's murder became known, Whiteley and Guenther immediately saw similarities to the Hinman case. The proximity of the murders in time and place and the similarity of the mode of death set off an alarm in the minds of the sheriff's deputies. After checking with law enforcement officials, Whiteley and Guenther learned an important detail about the Tate-LaBianca slayings that had not yet surfaced in the media: At each of the murder scenes the killer or killers had scrawled words in blood on the walls of the victims' homes. At the Tate home investigators found what appeared to be the word *pig*. At the LaBianca home, police found the words *death to pigs* and *HEALTER [Helter] SKELTER*. What only Whiteley, Guenther, and a handful of law enforcement officers knew was that words had also been printed on the wall of Gary Hinman's cabin. Someone had used Hinman's blood to spell out *political piggy*. Whiteley and Guenther decided to meet with the detectives investigating the Tate murder as soon as possible and inform them of this important clue.

On Sunday, August 10, Whiteley and Guenther drove to the Hall of Justice in downtown Los Angeles to meet with Sergeant

Jess Buckles, one of the LAPD detectives assigned to the Tate murders. Whiteley outlined the similarities of the murders in detail for Buckles, saving the biggest news for last: The sheriff's office had arrested a suspect in the case. On August 6 a man driving one of the stolen cars belonging to Gary Hinman was arrested. The suspect had blood on his shirt and trousers, and the arresting officers found a knife hidden in the tire well of his car. The sheriff's deputies had booked the driver of the car, Bobby Beausoleil, on suspicion of murder. Beausoleil, an actor and an amateur musician, was almost certainly involved in the murder of

When the Los Angeles Police Department ignored the Bobby Beausoleil (center) lead, the investigation was set back several months.

Hinman—a murder with a number of striking similarities to those Buckles was investigating. Surely, this must be the lead that Buckles and his colleagues were looking for, Whiteley thought.

To Whiteley's surprise, Buckles was not impressed. If Beausoleil had been arrested on August 6, Buckles reasoned, he could not be a suspect in the murder of Sharon Tate, which occurred three days later. Whitely agreed, but he explained that Beausoleil had been living in a hippie commune with dozens of others when arrested. Perhaps one of the commune members was connected to the Tate killings. It was definitely worth further investigation. Buckles scoffed at the notion that hippies were involved in the murder. "Naw, we know what's behind these murders. They're part of a big dope transaction."[8] Buckles told Whiteley that he would pass the tip on to his superiors and get back to him, but the detective did neither. His decision set the investigation back several months.

The next day, August 11, the Tate investigators released the man who had been their prime—and only—suspect. After questioning William Garretson and giving him a lie-detector test, the police were forced to concede that the young groundskeeper was not involved in the multiple murders. That evening LAPD authorities announced that Garretson was no longer a suspect in the case. Little did the LAPD know that it would be nearly four months before it would have another legitimate suspect.

The Investigation Stalls

Worldwide fascination with the murders grew with each passing day, and feeding the public's morbid appetite for details of the crime became nearly a full-time endeavor for many of the country's magazines and newspapers. Tabloid newspapers published every new rumor as fact. Television talk shows hosted a parade of so-called experts who claimed insight into the murders. Movie studios, hoping to capitalize on the publicity, rushed to re-release any movie that featured Sharon Tate. Calls and tips poured into police headquarters.

Through all of this, the LAPD maintained that the murders of the LaBiancas and of Sharon Tate and her houseguests were unrelated. A team of four officers was assigned to the Tate murders. A separate group of officers worked on the LaBianca killings. The murder of Gary Hinman, which fell outside the jurisdiction of the LAPD, was ignored. The two teams of investigators pursued separate leads, interviewed separate witnesses, and filed separate progress reports. For months the two teams were even reluctant to share information.

Critics of the department spoke of jealousy and rivalries between the two teams. Furthermore, the investigation was plagued by shortsightedness and inflexibility. The police department still saw the crimes as robberies and shaped their investigations along those lines. Because investigators had found illegal drugs at the Polanski house, the Tate team maintained its stance that the murders at Cielo Drive were tied to a drug operation.

As the weeks passed, pressure on the police department grew. Hounded by the media and the public for progress in the case, the police held press conferences merely to discount rumors and false leads and rehash old evidence. By the two-month anniversary of the murders, the updates from the LAPD had virtually ceased. Cynics suggested that the reports had stopped because the LAPD had nothing to report.

A Break in the Case

Although the murder investigation at the LAPD had stalled, the sheriff's office continued to make progress in the Hinman case. Sheriffs from Inyo County, California, a remote and sparsely populated area near Death Valley National Monument, had contacted Sergeants Whiteley and Guenther with a strange discovery. Their department had recently raided a suspected stolen car operation at desolate Barker Ranch. Officers had been staked out near the ranch in darkness, waiting for the signal to start the dawn raid. Suddenly, two terrified teenage girls emerged from the brush near the ranch. They told the officers that they had been living at Barker Ranch with a large group that called itself "the Family." The girls had been growing increasingly frightened with the illegal activities going on at the ranch and were attempting to leave. They said that men armed with shotguns were

"THE LOVE HOUSE"

When Sharon Tate and Roman Polanski moved into the ranch-style home at 10050 Cielo Drive, the young actress named it "the Love House." The house had a history of happiness, friends told Tate. Actress Candice Bergen and her boyfriend, music producer Terry Melcher, had made a home there. Before them, actor Henry Fonda lived in the house, and even earlier Cary Grant and Randolph Scott had shared the home during the golden age of Hollywood. But after August 9, 1969, the house on the street whose name was Spanish for *heaven* would never know happiness again.

Owner Rudi Altobelli, who rented the home to the Polanskis, lived in the guest quarters of the home after the murders, but the main home stood vacant for years. The home was listed on street vendors' maps to the movie stars' homes for decades. Altobelli hired round-the-clock security to guard the home from vandals and curiosity seekers. Even changing the house's street number did not fool the sightseers.

After Altobelli sold the house, the new owners used it as a rental property. The home once again came to the public's attention when Brian Warner, a rock musician whose stage name is Marilyn Manson, leased the home, installed recording equipment, and recorded songs containing lyrics by Charles Manson. Soon, real estate firms began to refuse to list the home. Finally, in 1994, the owners razed the home and rebuilt on the property. Even in destruction, the house could not escape infamy: Bricks and rubble from the home were soon being offered for sale on the Internet.

By contrast, the house at 3301 Waverly Drive, the former home of Leno and Rosemary LaBianca, never commanded the kind of notoriety that plagued the house on Cielo Drive. Although movie mogul Walt Disney once lived at the house, there is little in the past or present to draw

the morbid or curious to the property. The owner reports that she has lived there comfortably for decades and intends to pass the home on to her daughter at a future date.

The house at 10050 Cielo Drive.

searching for them, trying to keep them from escaping. The sheriffs took the girls into protective custody.

The runaway girls identified themselves as Stephanie Schram and Kitty Lutesinger. Lutesinger's name seemed familiar to one of the deputies who handled the girls' case. He called Whiteley and asked if he was looking for a girl with that name in connection with the murder of Gary Hinman. Whiteley verified that he was. He and Guenther immediately drove the 225 miles to interview the young woman.

Lutesinger's Story

Whiteley and Guenther were interested in Lutesinger because they believed she was the girlfriend of Bobby Beausoleil, the prime suspect in the Hinman murder case. During the interview Lutesinger admitted to the relationship. She said that a few months earlier, at Beausoleil's urging, she had dropped out of high school and left home to live with him in a hippie commune located at Spahn Ranch, on the outskirts of Los Angeles. Shortly afterward, however, Beausoleil had disappeared. Lutesinger had heard rumors that he was in jail, but the other members of the commune would not give her any information. Later, when Lutesinger had heard that Charles Manson, the leader of the Family, was planning to move the commune to a new location, she decided that she would leave the group.

After the Family moved to Barker Ranch, Lutesinger and her friend Stephanie Schram announced that they were leaving. Their plans were not acceptable to the group, however, which viewed leaving as an act of treason, punishable by death. The girls tried to escape anyway. The officers who had found the two girls in the desert had rescued them from pursuers who were intent on carrying out the death sentences.

After listening to Lutesinger's story, Whiteley confirmed her suspicions that her boyfriend had been arrested. He told her that Beausoleil had been arrested for the murder of Hinman and would almost certainly be convicted. Whiteley then asked Lutesinger if she knew anything about the murder. The frightened girl then did what the other Manson Family members had feared she might. She told the detectives the rumors that had circulated among the Family at the ranch after Beausoleil's disappearance. Lutesinger had heard that Manson had sent Beausoleil and two girls to Hinman's home to demand money from him and that a fight had broken out. Lutesinger said she had heard that Hinman was killed. She knew that at least one of the Family members had accompanied Beausoleil to Hinman's cabin. Her name was Sadie, Lutesinger said, and she was crazy.

Crazy or not, Sadie was someone the detectives wanted to interview. If she was at the scene when Gary Hinman was killed, the detectives knew that she had information about the murder. What they did not know was that talking with Sadie would solve the Tate-LaBianca murders as well.

Chapter 2

Confession and Capture

S ADIE, DETECTIVES FOUND OUT, was the nickname of Manson Family member Susan Atkins. As they suspected, Atkins knew a great deal about the Gary Hinman murder. She not only admitted to being present at the killing but also to participating in it. Atkins would later retract her confession, but not before it had led the police to the Tate-LaBianca murderers.

Atkins had been with the Manson Family much longer than Kitty Lutesinger and Stephanie Schram. On her own since she was fifteen, Atkins had spent six years traveling up and down the West Coast before meeting Charles Manson and joining his group. By then, Atkins already had a criminal record. She had been jailed on charges of robbery, possession of illegal drugs, and aggravated assault against a police officer. When Sergeants Whiteley and Guenther tracked down Atkins, she was in police custody again, arrested during the raid on Barker Ranch.

Whiteley and Guenther interviewed Atkins on October 13, 1969, almost three months after Hinman's death. Despite her record, the twenty-one-year-old prisoner did not strike Whiteley and Guenther as a sophisticated criminal. As Atkins answered their questions, she seemed unconcerned about implicating herself in Hinman's murder. Whiteley and Guenther sat amazed as Atkins laid out the details of Hinman's death. Hinman owed Manson money, Atkins said, so she, Bobby Beausoleil, and another girl named Mary Brunner went with Manson to Hinman's cabin and demanded payment. When Hinman did not cooperate, Manson took out a sword he had brought with him and struck Hinman on the head, slicing off one of his ears. The bleeding

Susan Atkins seemed unconcerned about implicating herself when she boasted about her part in the Hinman murder.

Hinman insisted he had no money to give them. Manson ordered his three accomplices not to leave Hinman's house until they had gotten money from him. Manson left, Atkins said, while she, Beausoleil, and Brunner remained at the cabin for two more days, torturing and taunting Hinman. Finally convinced that they were not going to get any money, Beausoleil stabbed Hinman to death. The killers drew on the walls with Hinman's blood, locked the cabin, and left. Atkins finished her account by admitting that she and her accomplices stole Hinman's two cars and drove back to the Manson Family's commune at Spahn Ranch.

Dumbstruck by Atkins's candor, officers asked the young woman if she would repeat her story on tape. She refused. Nevertheless, the officers quickly arranged to transfer Atkins to Los Angeles's Sybil Brand Women's Correctional Facility, where she was charged with the murder of Gary Hinman.

An Unusual Cell Mate

Atkins's willingness—and even eagerness—to talk about herself and her crimes was not limited to the interrogation room. She also regaled her cell mates with stories about her criminal life.

At the Sybil Brand Women's Correctional Facility, Atkins shared a cell with inmates Virginia Graham and Ronnie Howard. The two women, both in their thirties, had each served considerable time in prison in the past. Graham was back in custody for violating parole, and Howard was in jail for forging prescriptions. Graham and Howard had known each other outside of prison. Since they were assigned to the same prison dormitory, they had plenty of time for conversation. They talked of mutual acquaintances, their troubles with the law, and about Atkins, the new prisoner who had recently joined them in Dormitory 8000.

Graham and Howard agreed that neither of them had ever known an inmate as peculiar as Susan Atkins. She was very young, for one thing, and seemed far too carefree, considering her surroundings. She would burst into song or break into giggles at any moment, and she never stopped talking. At the end of the day, the three inmates would sit on their bunks and Sadie—as Atkins insisted on being called—would talk and talk. She told her two cell mates about her experiences with illegal drugs, her criminal history, and her open marriage in a commune with dozens of other men and women her age.

Charlie

Atkins's favorite subject was Charlie, a musician who was the head of the commune. Atkins told her cellmates that he was the most powerful man she had ever met. He had been in jail many times, but he had emerged from prison unbroken. He could read minds, Atkins claimed, and had taught her to play the guitar in just one lesson. Charlie's own singing and playing left her spellbound, Atkins declared. She recalled for Graham and Howard the first time she heard Charlie's music, "I knew immediately that he might be God Himself. If not God Himself, then very close to God."[9] As if to verify her remark, Atkins explained that Charlie's

A FRESH START FAILS

In 1949 Charles Manson left Indiana for Boys Town, the famous boys orphanage, where authorities hoped the boy might make a clean start. Manson was accepted into Boys Town with the help of Father George Powers, a Catholic priest who came to know Manson, then living in the Indiana Juvenile Detention Center. The priest recognized Manson's intelligence and held out hope that he might be straightened out with guidance and love. Father Powers later recalled in Robert Newell's article "Dream Comes True for Lad; He's Going to Boys Town" that

> he attracted my attention because he didn't have anyone who ever came to see him or cared much about him, so I took over and tried to be sort of a daddy, I guess. And he certainly had a great need for people in his life. So I'd take him over to my own mother's house—she remembers him very well as a kid who sort of followed her around the house and when she was fixing supper, he'd be standing right there waiting to help her. He was a very dependent type, who craved attention and affection. And he never got it, except in anti-social ways. . . . He didn't have too many people that cared for him. That's the whole thing. They didn't care if he lived or died. We had hoped that maybe he could start a whole new life with a kind of family in Nebraska [Boys Town].

Instead of finding a new life in Nebraska, Manson found a friend named Blackie Nielson, who would become his partner in crime. The two boys stole a car and traveled across three states, committing several burglaries before being arrested. After this arrest, no one interceded for Manson. He was sent to the Indiana School for Boys.

full name was Charles Manson, a play on the words *man's son* or *son of man*—the words often used to describe Jesus Christ. As proof of Manson's supernatural nature, Atkins offered another incident:

One night, we were high on grass, and I looked at Charlie across the room. Men were clustered around him. I counted the men; there were twelve. With his hair and beard, his eyes staring intently from face to face, he looked like Jesus talking to the twelve apostles. The thought thrilled me. I thought he might be Christ.[10]

Atkins finished the story with a prediction: Manson would rescue her from prison. She warned her cell mates that America would soon be in flames as the result of a cataclysmic race war. The black race would rise up and kill all of the members of white society, Manson had said. In the resulting chaos, Manson would assume power and reign as commander of the entire world. Atkins believed that before the tumult, which Manson had named Helter Skelter, Manson would rescue her and take her and the rest of his Family to an underground paradise hidden in the California desert. Graham and Howard had no idea what to make of any of Atkins's outlandish stories. But Atkins's strangest tale was yet to come.

"First-Degree Murder"

Graham and Atkins shared work duty during the day in the prison office. One day Graham asked Atkins why she was in prison. Atkins's reply was quick. "You know—first degree murder,"[11] Atkins said. Surprised at the blunt answer, Graham asked Atkins if she had really committed the crime. Graham expected a denial, but instead Atkins admitted her guilt.

Over the next hour Atkins described the torture and murder of Gary Hinman. Atkins told of the murder, Graham later recalled, as if "it was the most perfectly natural thing to do."[12] Atkins had not finished her shocking confession, however. She asked Graham if she had heard about the murders at Roman Polanski's house. Of course, Graham had. Atkins asked if she knew who had committed the bloody crime. When Graham shook her head, Atkins beamed: "Well, you're looking at her!"[13] Still skeptical, Graham pressed Atkins for details, admitting that she was curious about the crime. Atkins obliged. Graham became the first person outside the Manson Family to hear the complete story of the slaughter of Sharon Tate and her houseguests.

An Incredible Tale

Atkins said that she and three other members of the Family— Tex Watson, Patricia Krenwinkel, and Linda Kasabian—left Spahn Ranch at about midnight on Friday, August 8. On Manson's orders, they were dressed in dark clothes, and each carried a hunting knife. Watson also had a gun. Their destination was

Police examine the car in which Steven Parent was murdered at the Tate house.

10050 Cielo Drive. Watson was familiar with the layout of the house and grounds because both he and Manson had been to the house when previous tenants had lived there. Manson picked the house because it was isolated. The killers parked their car outside the fence and, after Watson severed the phone line, they scaled the walls to the grounds of the home.

Steven Parent was the first to die. Watson shot him as he sat in a car in the driveway near the caretaker's house, where he had been visiting William Garretson. While Kasabian kept watch outside, Watson, Atkins, and Krenwinkel slipped into the house through a window. Once inside, the murderers gathered everyone into the living room. Jay Sebring made a rush for Watson's gun, but Watson shot him in the chest. After Sebring fell to the floor, Watson stabbed him. Krenwinkel turned to Gibby Folger and stabbed her. Folger managed to run out to the front lawn before she collapsed and died. Voytek Frykowski also died outside the house. Sharon Tate was the last to be killed. Atkins said that

TEX WATSON MEETS HIS MASTER

Charles "Tex" Watson was Manson's most trusted assistant and the Family member who shed the most blood in the Tate-LaBianca murders. In *Will You Die For Me?*, Watson's book about his days with the Family, he recalls his first meeting with Manson.

It began one night when I was driving out Sunset Boulevard toward the beach, heading home to Malibu. Hitchhikers were pretty common on Sunset, and I pulled over to pick one up. When he told me his name was Dennis Wilson it didn't mean anything to me, but when he said he was one of the Beach Boys I was impressed. . . . When we got to his house in Pacific Palisades he invited me in. . . . There he (Manson) was surrounded by five or six girls, on the floor next to the huge coffee table with a guitar in his hands. He looked up, and the first thing I felt was a sort of gentleness, an embracing kind of acceptance and love.

Suddenly the girls came out of the kitchen and started serving us sandwiches they'd made—organic, full of sprouts and avocado and cheese. It was as if we were kings, just because we were men, and nothing could make them happier than waiting on us, making us happy. We all lay back and listened to Charlie sing to us about love. . . . I'd never known such peace.

Tex Watson on his way to court.

Late that night at my truck as I was leaving, Dennis smiled and told me to come by anytime, take a swim in the pool, whatever I wanted. I drove out to Malibu, knowing that whatever had been going wrong in my life would be okay now. I'd found what really mattered: love between people, love that made all the old ideas about love as romance—or love as your parents pushing at you—just fade away. Charlie Manson was the first person I'd met who really knew what love was all about.

the actress had begged for her life and for the life of her baby, but Watson and Atkins showed no mercy, stabbing her in the chest until she died. Atkins then told Graham the most gruesome detail of all. She claimed that she had tasted Sharon Tate's blood and wrote on the door with it.

Back in Dormitory 8000, Graham took Ronnie Howard aside and relayed Atkins's incredible tale. Howard was skeptical. The murders were, of course, the most talked about crime in America, and Howard reasoned that Atkins could have simply been repeating things she had read in the newspaper. Graham and Howard made a pledge to find out more about the murders from Atkins and then compare notes to see if Atkins changed her story. The two prisoners never got a chance to test the consistency of Atkins's account, however. A few days after hearing Atkins's incredible confession, Virginia Graham was transferred from Sybil Brand to another women's prison. As she left, Graham told Howard that she would have to proceed on her own. Howard promised her friend that she would, but she was not sure that she had the courage to bring up the subject with the self-proclaimed killer.

Howard did not have to worry about how to bring up the subject of murder, though. Her talkative cell mate brought up the subject herself. Not long after Graham was transferred out, Howard made the offhand remark that nothing could surprise her anymore. Atkins could not resist the opening. She claimed that she could tell Howard something that would surprise and shock her. She asked Howard if she had heard about the murder victim who had been found with a fork stuck in his stomach. When Howard said she had, Atkins bragged that she and her friends had committed the murder. She also claimed that the Manson Family had plans to kill more celebrities and politicians.

A Difficult Decision

Howard had a difficult decision to make. She had never informed on another criminal in the past, and she did not wish to begin doing so. At the same time, she was convinced that the Manson Family was capable of killing more people on its hit list. "I kept thinking that if I didn't say anything these people (Manson's followers) would probably be set free," she later recalled. "They were going to pick other houses. . . . I just couldn't see all those innocent people being killed."[14] In the end, Howard decided to tell the authorities what she knew.

Ronnie Howard, Susan Atkins's cell mate, informed on her and testified against her in court.

Although Howard had overcome her own misgivings about informing on her cell mate, she still faced an unexpected obstacle: No one would listen to her. The prison guards whom Howard approached with the story did not believe her because her version of the events did not match what the guards had read in the newspapers. On November 17, 1969, Ronnie Howard was taken out of prison for an appearance in court. Desperate to tell authorities what she knew, Howard dashed to a pay telephone. She dialed the Beverly Hills Police Station and asked to speak to a homicide detective. When one came on the line, she blurted out that she knew who had committed the Sharon Tate murders. The detective told Howard that the Tate case was being handled by the Hollywood Police Station and suggested she call there. Howard frantically dialed the second number, but by the time she reached a homicide detective, she was being summoned to leave for court. She gave the detective her name, told him she knew who had committed the Tate murders, said that she was an inmate at the Sybil Brand facility, and hung up without knowing if the police had taken her seriously.

They had. Later that evening two officers from the LAPD drove out to Sybil Brand to follow up on Howard's claim. When they heard Howard's account of the crime, the officers immediately realized they had a valuable witness—one who was too important to return to the prison population. They put Howard in protective custody and returned to police headquarters with the startling news.

Another Tip

When the officers arrived back at police headquarters they found their colleagues interrogating Danny DeCarlo, a member of the Straight Satans motorcycle club. DeCarlo was suspected of dealing in stolen automobile parts. Their questions had led to a strange story from the motorcyclist. Among the motley figures he knew within the illicit car parts trade was a "guru" named Charles Manson, who ran a large hippie commune at Spahn Ranch. Manson had tried numerous times to recruit members of the Straight Satans into his communal family. The Manson group was gathering weapons in anticipation of the end of the world, DeCarlo told the policemen. Once during a visit to the commune, a member of Manson's Family had bragged to DeCarlo about killing five "piggies," or members of the law-abiding community. It had occurred to DeCarlo that maybe the reference was to the Sharon Tate murders.

After hearing the stories of Howard and DeCarlo on November 17, the LAPD detectives focused the investigation on the Manson Family. Atkins was the first to be charged. Her case was assigned to Deputy District Attorneys Aaron Stovitz and his thirty-five-year-old colleague Vincent Bugliosi. Stovitz was eventually moved off the case. For Bugliosi, however, the prosecution of the Manson Family became a full-time endeavor for nearly two years.

The Prosecutors Make a Deal

Bugliosi's first order of business was to interview Susan Atkins. Atkins had hired attorney Richard Caballero to represent her in the Hinman murder; now Caballero would have the added task of defending her against the Tate-LaBianca charges. Caballero met with Bugliosi and listened as the deputy district attorney outlined the state's evidence in the case against his client. At the end of the briefing, Caballero was convinced that the evidence was strong enough to convict Atkins. After conferring with his client, Caballero asked for immunity, or freedom from criminal charges, for Atkins in exchange for her testimony against Manson and the other members of the Family. The district attorney's office opposed the deal because the prosecutors did not want to see a murderer go free. Instead, they offered a compromise: They would charge Atkins for murder, but in exchange for her cooperation, they would not seek the death penalty against her.

Deputy District Attorney Vincent Bugliosi spent nearly two years in the spotlight while prosecuting the case.

Under California law, the first step for the prosecutors in a criminal case is to present the evidence of criminal wrongdoing to a grand jury. The panel of jurors must then decide if the evidence presented is strong enough for criminal charges to be made against the suspects. On Friday, December 5, Atkins took the stand in front of the grand jury. Twenty-one jurors listened to her emotionless account of the five murders committed at the home of Sharon Tate and the two murders committed at the home of Leno and Rosemary LaBianca. Led by Bugliosi's questions, Atkins spoke frankly about the multiple murders. To the jurors, it appeared that Atkins was truthful. She did not, however, appear to feel any remorse for what she had done.

More Witnesses

After Atkins finished testifying, Bugliosi and Stovitz called three more witnesses to the stand—Wilfred Parent, the father of Steven Parent; Winifred Chapman, the housekeeper who had reported the murders; and Terry Melcher, a music producer who had previously owned the home at Cielo Drive and had once given Charles Manson an audition for a recording contract. When the day's testimony was complete, court was adjourned until the following Monday. When the hearing resumed on December 8, Bugliosi and Stovitz called several more witnesses—police officers who had gathered evidence, medical examiners who had performed autopsies on the victims, and others. Less than twenty minutes after beginning deliberations, the grand jury returned murder indictments against Susan Atkins, Charles Manson, Patricia Krenwinkel, Charles "Tex" Watson, Leslie Van Houten, and Linda Kasabian.

The police tracked Tex Watson to his boyhood home in Texas. They found Krenwinkel with relatives in Alabama. Kasabian was arrested at her mother's home in New Hampshire. All were ordered to return to California to stand trial. However, Watson fought extradition for several months. As a result, he would eventually be tried separately from the other Manson Family defendants. Manson, the accused mastermind behind the murders, was not hard to find. He was already in jail; in fact, he had been arrested and jailed twice since the murders. The weekend after the murders, he was arrested at Spahn Ranch on grand theft auto charges, only to be released on a technicality. On October 12 Manson had been arrested again during the police raid on Barker Ranch. He was being held in the tiny town of Independence, California, on charges of vandalism and arson. The police in Independence gladly handed Manson over to the Los Angeles authorities. The suspect was transported from Inyo to Los Angeles County under extremely heavy guard, and on December 11, when he was brought before Judge William Keene, hundreds of reporters and photographers were on hand to witness the arraignment.

A Sense of Relief

After Manson was booked into custody, many Southern Californians—and people across the country—felt relieved. Citizens and public officials congratulated the LAPD on a job well done. The widespread belief was that convictions of the murderers were a foregone conclusion. Vincent Bugliosi knew otherwise. He later observed,

> Neither the finding, the arresting, nor the indicting of a defendant has evidentiary value and none are proof of guilt. Once the killer is identified, there remains the difficult (and sometimes insurmountable) problem of connecting him to the crime with strong, admissible evidence—then proving his guilt beyond a reasonable doubt, be it before a judge or jury. And as yet we hadn't even made the first step, much less the second.[15]

Although the evidence against Charles Manson and his followers was great, the prosecution still had gaps in its case that had to be filled in if all defendants were to be found guilty.

Chapter 3

The Case Against the Manson Family

THE LOS ANGELES COUNTY DISTRICT Attorney's Office faced a much more difficult situation after the capture of the Manson Family killers than the public realized. The indictments of the Manson Family rested on the confessions of Susan Atkins. Little physical evidence linked the killers to the scene of the crime. The gun used in the shootings had not been found. Few fingerprints had been left behind. Most importantly, the leader of the group, Charles Manson, had been nowhere near the murders when they occurred. He could be tried for conspiring to commit the crimes, but, due to safeguards in the legal system, the testimony of a co-conspirator such as Atkins by itself was not enough to convict him. To tie Manson to the murders, the prosecutors would have to offer clear proof that the murders were carried out as a direct result of Manson's orders.

Conspiracy

Since Manson had not killed anyone on August 8 or 9, he had been indicted under conspiracy laws. According to such laws, a person who plans or orders a murder is as responsible for the crime as the person who actually takes the victim's life. Vincent Bugliosi later explained,

> The heart of our case against Manson was the "vicarious liability" rule of conspiracy—each conspirator is criminally responsible for all the crimes committed by his co-

conspirators if said crimes were committed to further the object of the conspiracy. This rule applies even if the conspirator was not present at the scene of the crime. For example: A, B and C decide to rob a bank. 'A' plans the robbery, 'B' and 'C' carry it out. Under the law, 'A,' though he never entered the bank, is as responsible as 'B' and 'C.'[16]

But although conspiracy laws gave the prosecution grounds for charging Manson with the Tate-LaBianca murders, the court's interpretation of these laws made proving conspiracy extremely difficult. One legal safeguard in particular—a 1965 ruling known as the Aranda rule—did not allow the testimony of one conspirator to be used as evidence against another conspirator without some other evidence to corroborate, or verify, the testimony. The Aranda rule meant that as damaging as Atkins's grand jury testimony had been, the state could not use her statements as the only evidence against Manson. Knowing this, Paul Fitzgerald, the head of the defense team, told reporters, "There is no case against Manson."[17] Some legal insiders predicted that the charges against Manson would be dropped due to a lack of evidence.

The New Rasputin

To prove conspiracy, the prosecution had to show that Manson controlled the actions of his Family members. The father of Susan Atkins said in interviews that he believed that Manson held magical powers over his daughter. Joseph Krenwinkel recalled how his daughter, Patricia, left with Manson within hours of meeting him, not even bothering to pick up her paycheck at work. "I am convinced he was some kind of hypnotist,"[18] Krenwinkel said. Stories in the press compared Manson to Rasputin, the sinister mystic who was reputed to have had a psychological grip on Russia's royal family during the nineteenth century.

Domination

Bugliosi agreed that Manson exerted a powerful influence over his followers, but he knew that he could not prove Manson's guilt by portraying his power as mystical or supernatural. Mysticism

MANSON THE MANIPULATOR

Manson's mysterious power to persuade has always been a subject of intrigue. Writer Nuel Emmons worked with Manson on the book *Charles Manson: In His Own Words*. While gathering material for the book, Emmons, along with another writer, visited Manson in prison. Manson's exchanges with the female journalist gave Emmons insight into Manson's techniques as a manipulator.

At first Manson virtually ignored the woman, but as he showed us his photo album . . . he became a charmer. The interviewer was in her late twenties, neither a beauty nor homely, but by the time Manson had talked to her for a while, she must have believed she was the most attractive woman on earth. . . .

When he spoke to her he was polite, courteous and complimentary. His normal profanity and prison slang had disappeared, and in fact, he was more articulate than I would have believed possible. Very soon he was holding her hand and caressing the skin of her bare arm while she listened intently to every word he said.

He stood up and began massaging the back of the interviewer's neck and shoulders. She closed her eyes and smiled appreciatively. Then, continuing the conversation, he casually reached across the table and picked up the cord of the tape recorder we were using. He looked at me and winked. Suddenly and menacingly, he wrapped the cord around the woman's neck. Her eyes opened wide, filling her glasses, and she looked at me pleadingly. Manson applied some pressure on the cord and in an intimidating voice said, "Whatta ya think . . . should I take this little b——'s life?"

The woman was terrified, and . . . the pressure of the cord on the woman's neck gave me cause for a moment's real concern. Just as I was contemplating a rescue effort, he laughed and loosened the cord, saying, "See . . . you never want to trust a stranger."

might make interesting newspaper copy, but it would not stand up to argument in a court of law. A guilty verdict depended on rational, verifiable facts. Bugliosi had to show that Manson had used scientifically accepted mind-control techniques to control the behavior of his followers. As Bugliosi later explained,

Put yourself in the jury box. Would you believe the prosecutor if he told you that a little runt . . . sent some half dozen people, the majority of them young girls, out to murder for him, their victims not persons they knew or had a grudge against, but complete strangers, including a pregnant woman, and that without argument they did it? To convince a jury of [Manson's responsibility in the murders] . . . (we) would first have to convince them of Manson's domination over the Family, and particularly over his co-defendants. A domination so total, so complete that they would do anything he told them to do. Including murder."[19]

The prosecution found that Manson used a combination of elements contained in the popular phrase of the day—sex, drugs, and rock and roll—to weaken the independence of his followers and assert his dominance over them.

The Manson Family was a free-love commune. All of the members were encouraged to have sex with each other to break down traditional barriers and increase the unity of the group.

Manson's followers were intensely loyal and came to court every day during the trial. A Family member draws a sketch of Manson for the benefit of the press.

Since Manson was the leader of the group, his sexual attention was desired by many of the female family members. Through sex, Manson created strong bonds and loyalties among his followers and diminished their independence.

Drugs were available at the commune as well, especially marijuana and LSD. The drugs tended to weaken the critical faculties of the Family members, making them more open to Manson's theories and predictions and more susceptible to his suggestions. Under the influence of drugs, Manson's followers remained unaware of the more dangerous aspects of their existence.

A musician and songwriter, Manson attracted many of his followers through his singing and guitar playing. At the commune

HIPPIES AND VIOLENCE

During the late 1960s hippies celebrated their group identity as peaceful and loving people. Although the hippie lifestyle was condemned as irresponsible by many members of mainstream society, few viewed hippies as dangerous. The emergence of the Manson Family as vicious killers shocked America and left many people wondering how the hippie lifestyle could spawn such antisocial acts. After the arrests of Manson and his followers, a *Time* magazine article entitled "Hippies and Violence: The Demon of Death Valley" included an interview with Dr. Lewis Yablonsky who offered this analysis of hippie culture.

Part of the mystique and the attraction of the hippie movement has always been its invitation to freedom. It beckons young people out of the tense, structured, workaday world to a life where each can do "his own thing." . . . It has drawn all sorts of people: the rebellious, the lonely, the poets, the disaffected, and worse. . . .

A few of them, like Manson, also found other advantages to being a hippie. The true gentle folk were relatively defenseless. Leaderless, they responded readily to strong leaders. But how could children who had dropped out for the sake of kindness and sharing, love and beauty, be enjoined to kill? [Dr. Lewis] Yablonsky thinks that the answer may lie in the fact that so many hippies are actually "lonely, alienated people." He says, "They have had so few love models that even when they act as if they love, they can be totally void of true compassion. That is the reason why they can kill so matter of factly."

his strange, rambling improvisations added to his mystique as a guru and a prophet. In addition, Manson came to believe that other musicians—mainly the Beatles—were communicating with him through their music. In particular, Manson believed that several songs on the Beatles' *White Album*, including "Helter Skelter," "Blackbird," "Piggies," "Happiness Is a Warm Gun," and "Revolution #9," pointed to an impending revolution. By linking his predictions to songs by the world's most popular musical group, Manson was able to convince Family members that he was in touch with a large, worldwide movement. To reinforce his special knowledge and power, Manson ordered the *White Album* to be played around the clock at the commune.

In addition to such peaceful means of influencing his followers, Manson also used terror and fear. Manson's apocalyptic vision was based not on love and peace but on hate and violence. The race war and his ensuing ascent to power would be bloody. No one in the Family doubted Manson's willingness to use violence to promote his goals. Those who crossed the Family were dealt with harshly. Manson used violence and threats to maintain his domination within the family as well.

Key Witness

In December 1969 the prosecution at last found another witness who could testify about Manson's use of violence and his domination over his Family—or, rather, the witness found the prosecution. That month Manson Family member Linda Kasabian returned from New Hampshire and surrendered to authorities at Sybil Brand prison. Kasabian admitted to having driven the killers to and from both murder scenes and offered to tell everything she knew about the murders.

At first Kasabian seemed a risky witness for the prosecution. She claimed that she had not participated in the killing but had only driven the getaway car—an account that seemed self-serving. By her own admission she had taken hundreds of drug trips and had love affairs with every man at the commune at one time or another. She had once believed herself to be a witch, and she acknowledged that she had been "completely in love with Charlie"[20]

Linda Kasabian, a Family member, became Bugliosi's star witness in court.

before the murders. Bugliosi wanted to get to know Kasabian before he took a chance at putting her before a jury. Under complete secrecy, Bugliosi walked into Sybil Brand prison to meet the girl who was to become his star witness.

Bugliosi had met and talked with at least a dozen Manson Family women since he had started working on the case. The women in custody were often contemptuous of him. Those who were not involved in the murders but stood vigil near the jail and courthouse struck Bugliosi as either deceitful or blissfully naive. Bugliosi found Linda Kasabian to be none of these things. An expectant mother, Kasabian was polite, attentive, and even demure. She alone among the Manson Family members seemed to realize the tragic dimension of the case. Bugliosi later recalled that Kasabian had the sad look of someone with a broken heart.

Kasabian spoke openly and fully about her life with the Manson Family. She described the nights of the murders in detail and told of her escape from Spahn Ranch. She displayed a clear sense that terrible things had been done by her former friends, including Manson. Her willingness to testify in court against Manson struck Bugliosi as particularly brave. Kasabian offered to accompany the investigators to the scenes of the crimes, if necessary. Her account of life in the Family confirmed Manson's role in the planning of the murder, his domination of the group, and his control over his followers. When Bugliosi returned to his office and reviewed the tape recordings made during the interrogation, he was impressed to discover that Kasabian did not contradict herself or refuse to answer any question. Bugliosi decided that she would make a good witness. On February 28 he signed documents promising Kasabian immunity on all charges in exchange for her testimony.

Additional Evidence

Although the prosecution had obtained testimony against the Manson Family defendants, it had little physical evidence that linked the defendants to the crimes. In December 1969 this changed, largely because of an article that ran in the *Los Angeles Times*.

On Sunday, December 14, the *Los Angeles Times* featured a front-page article titled "Susan Atkins' Story of Two Nights of Murder," which was based on the account of the murders that Atkins had given to her attorney. The story included a description of the type of pistol the police believed had been used in the murders but had never been found. The story caught the eye of a coworker of Bernard Weiss, whose son, Stephen, had found a similar pistol three months earlier. While fixing a sprinkler in the backyard bushes of his

Ten-year-old Stephen Weiss became an instant media celebrity after finding the murder weapon in his backyard.

family's Sherman Oaks home on September 1, ten-year-old Stephen spotted a gun lying on the ground. The revolver's long barrel was bent, and the handle was smashed, but Stephen knew to be careful. He picked the gun up gently by the tip of the barrel, walked to the house, and showed the weapon to his father, who immediately called the police. A police officer stopped at the Weiss home, picked up the gun, and returned it to police headquarters. Because the weapon was found miles from the sites of the Tate-LaBianca murders, no one at the police headquarters connected the gun to the August murders. When Bernard Weiss's coworker told him about the story in the *Los Angeles Times*, Weiss immediately read the article and recognized the weapon as the type his son had found in their backyard. It took five calls before Weiss could get his story heard, but finally investigators located the forgotten gun and entered it into evidence. Working with the bullets and the broken pieces of the gun's handle found at the scene, crime-lab workers were able to positively identify the gun as the one used in the murders.

At about the same time, investigators received another break. A local television news team tried to reenact the getaway described by Atkins in the *Los Angeles Times* article. The reporters drove the route street by street and even changed clothes along the way as Atkins said she and her companions had. At the moment they finished changing their clothes, the reporters pulled the car over and searched the shoulder of the road. At the bottom of a nearby embankment they were astonished at what they found: a bundle of bloody rags and clothes. They alerted the police, who came and retrieved the possible evidence. Laboratory tests later revealed that the bloody bundles were indeed the discarded clothing of the killers.

Also in December, crime-lab technicians were able to positively identify two fingerprints found at the Polanski home. The prints belonged to Tex Watson and Patricia Krenwinkel, proving their presence at the murder scene.

With solid physical evidence linking most of the defendants with the crime, the prosecution spent the remaining weeks before the trial preparing the case against the one defendant who was far from the crime scene on the night of the murders: Charles Manson. Bugliosi knew that he had to convince the jury that the plan to commit the murders had originated in Manson's mind. To do so, Bugliosi had to explain the motive, or reason, behind the murders.

Most murders are the result of strong personal emotions such as hatred, envy, fear, or greed. Other killers get a sexual or sadistic thrill out of taking another life. None of these motives seemed to apply to Manson, however. He could not have personal emotions about the victims since he did not know them. He could hardly derive a sexual or sadistic thrill from the killings since he was not present when they occurred. The motive behind the Tate-LaBianca murders was complex, impersonal, and bizarre.

THE WHITE ALBUM

Just in time for Christmas 1968, the Beatles released their twelfth record album, titled simply *The Beatles*. Because the album cover resembled a formal white invitation, Beatles fans and radio disc jockeys dubbed the recording the *White Album*. It quickly became the best-selling record in the world.

Manson played the *White Album* incessantly for the Family members during 1969. Manson told his disciples that he could decipher hidden meanings within its unusual and sometimes experimental songs. He told his followers that the Beatles were speaking to him personally through the music. The Beatles had put two songs on the album containing the word *revolution* in the titles. This was an obvious signal for a worldwide revolt, Manson claimed. The song titled "Piggies" showed the Beatles' hatred for the police and the rich, said Manson, while "Blackbird" warned of the revolution about to erupt among the nation's African American population. Most significant of all was the song "Helter Skelter." Manson claimed that it was the anthem of the imminent apocalypse, a reminder to the Family that it should prepare itself for the role that it would play after the holocaust.

At the beginning of the investigation, prosecutor Vincent Bugliosi was reluctant to use Manson's obsessions and delusions with the music as a motive in the Tate-LaBianca murders. But as he learned more and more about the emotional makeup of the Family, Bugliosi became convinced that the music and the paranoid worldview that Manson drew from it were a central part of the psychological hold that he held as the group's leader.

Helter Skelter

The murders arose from Manson's belief that a race war was about to occur in the United States. Deadly race riots had occurred in Los Angeles in 1965, in Detroit in 1967, and several other cities in 1968 following the assassination of Martin Luther King Jr. A few black leaders, including Huey P. Newton and Bobby Seal, founders of the Black Panthers, called for a violent revolution to replace the U.S. government and change the society they perceived as racist. Manson looked forward to such a race war, which he called Helter Skelter, because he believed that he could use it as a stepping-stone to power.

Manson believed that blacks would win the race war because they had been oppressed for centuries by whites and it was their turn to take over. A racist, Manson believed that blacks would not be capable of ruling their new nation by themselves. After a period of chaos—more Helter Skelter—the blacks would have to turn to the few whites who had survived for help. At that time, Manson and his family would emerge from hiding and take the reins of power.

Manson convinced his followers that the best way to bring about a new and better social order was to start the race war between blacks and whites. He believed the best way to do this was to commit a horrific murder in the white community, leaving evidence that would cause whites to think the crime was committed by blacks. This would turn the white community against the black community, and Helter Skelter would begin. This is the reason why, at Manson's instruction, the Tate-LaBianca killers wrote revolutionary code words such as *rise, pigs*, and *Helter Skelter* on the walls in the blood of the victims. Manson took these words from the lyrics of songs by the Beatles, whom Manson believed had communicated their own desire for Armageddon to him through their music.

Manson planned to survive Helter Skelter by hiding in a bottomless pit in the desert. This is why he moved the Family to the desert of Death Valley, the lowest point in North America. Manson based this decision on the words of Revelation 9, a chapter in

Manson moved his Family to the broken-down Spahn Ranch (pictured) in the desert in 1968. He planned eventually to move the Family to Death Valley, a good hiding place.

the last book of the New Testament, which Manson equated to "Revolution #9," a song by the Beatles. The bottomless pit, Manson told his followers, was a land of milk and honey with twelve types of fruit on every tree. Living in this earthly paradise, Manson said that his Family would grow to a population of 144,000.

Bugliosi realized that the Helter Skelter motive would be difficult for some jurors to accept, but he knew he would have to offer it for one simple reason: It was true. He later reflected,

> All the evidence we'd assembled thus far, I felt, pointed to one primary motive: Helter Skelter. It was far out, but then so were the murders themselves. It was admittedly bizarre, but from the first moment I was assigned to the case, I'd felt that for murders as bizarre as these the motive itself would have to be almost equally strange, not something you'd find within the pages of a textbook on police science.[21]

With a motive, physical evidence, and eyewitness testimony, the prosecution's case was complete. The question was whether a jury would believe it.

Chapter 4

A Bizarre Defense

F ACING A POSSIBLE CONVICTION that carried the death penalty, an experienced criminal like Charles Manson might have been expected to mount a vigorous defense aimed at impeaching, or discrediting, the evidence against him. After all, Manson was nowhere near Sharon Tate's home when the murders occurred there, and although he entered the LaBianca home and tied up Leno LaBianca with a leather thong, he had left the scene before the LaBiancas were killed. No physical evidence linked him with the crimes. The strongest evidence against him was the testimony of others about things he had told them to do.

Manson reasonably could have dismissed the Helter Skelter motive as nothing more than late-night ramblings designed to enthrall his followers. The idea that two sets of murders could trigger a nationwide race war that would leave Manson in charge of the United States was far-fetched, even for a self-styled guru. Because of the presumption of innocence, Manson did not have to prove any of these counter theories. All he had to do was create a reasonable doubt in the minds of the jurors that his words had been misunderstood.

To the surprise of many, Manson made only a halfhearted attempt to advance these arguments. Instead of mounting a credible defense, Manson chose to use his trial for a variety of purposes that had nothing to do with determining his guilt or innocence. Knowing that members of the media were hanging on his every word and gesture, Manson viewed the courtroom as a kind of public stage, a platform from which to accomplish a number of highly personal goals: to mock the legal system, to

Manson used the courtroom as a public stage to mock the legal system, to frighten the public, and to enhance his image as a mystical leader.

add to his notoriety, to frighten the public, and to enhance his image as a mystical leader. He knew that he could use his rights as a defendant to manipulate the legal system, to confound the prosecutors, slow the proceedings, and perhaps cause a mistrial. He decided to wage a one-man war not against the evidence but against the system that brought the evidence against him.

"I Have to Do It Myself"

Manson began his defense by asking the court to allow him to act in propria persona—as his own attorney. The U.S. Constitution guarantees this right to every citizen judged mentally competent. On December 17, 1969, nine days after being indicted for murder, Manson appeared before the presiding judge in his case,

William Keene, and requested that his public defender be dismissed. As a dropout of society—someone who rejected a traditional lifestyle—Manson did not believe he could be adequately represented by a member of the society that he had rejected:

> Your Honor, there is no way I can give up my voice in this matter. If I can't speak, then our whole thing is done. If I can't speak in my own defense and converse freely in this courtroom, then it ties my hands behind my back, and if I have no voice, then there is no sense in having a defense. . . . Lawyers play with people, and I am a person and I don't want to be played with in this matter. . . .There is no attorney in the world who can represent me as a person. I have to do it myself.[22]

Before Keene would rule on the request, he ordered Manson to meet with an independent attorney, Joseph Ball, a former president of the California State Bar Association, to discuss the issues associated with self-representation. Manson met with Ball in a private session on December 24. Ball reported back to Keene with his findings, saying that he found Manson to be

> an able, intelligent young man, quiet-spoken and mild-mannered. We went over different problems of law, and I found he had a ready understanding. . . . Remarkable understanding. As a matter of fact, he has a very fine brain. I complimented him on the fact. I think I told you that he had a high I.Q. Must have, to be able to converse as he did. And he feels that if he goes to trial and he is able to permit jurors and the Court to hear him and see him, they will realize he is not the kind of man who would perpetrate horrible crimes.[23]

Members of the prosecution believed that Manson had conned, or deceived, Ball, just as he had conned so many others. Bugliosi believed that Manson's move was just another example of his desire to control every aspect of his Family's life: "Manson's goal (was) to run the entire defense himself. In court as well as out, Charlie intended to retain complete control of the family."[24]

"I HAVE X'D MYSELF FROM YOUR WORLD"

When Charles Manson appeared in court for the first day of testimony in his murder trial, he bore a bloody X on his forehead. He had carved it there the night before to protest the judge's decision forbidding Manson to act as his own attorney. This written statement was distributed outside the courtroom by his disciples. It was reprinted in the *Los Angeles Free Press* in July of 1970.

I have **X**'d myself from your world. . . . I am not allowed to be a man in your society. I am considered inadequate and incompetent to speak or defend myself in your court. You have created the monster. I am not part of you, from you; nor do I condone your wars or your unjust attitudes towards things, animals and people.

I stand in the opposite to what you do and what you have done in the past. You have never given me the Constitution you speak of. The words you have used to trick the people are not mine. I do not accept what you call justice.

You! Look at what you have done and what you are doing. You make fun of God and have murdered the world in the name of Jesus Christ. I stand with my **X**, with my love, with my god and by myself. My faith in me is stronger than all your armies, governments, gas chambers or anything you may want to do to me. I know what you have done and your courtroom is man's game. Love is my judge. I have my own Constitution; it's inside me.

Manson carved an X in his forehead.

No man or lawyer is speaking for me. I speak for myself. I am not allowed to speak with words so I have spoken with the mark I will be wearing on my forehead. . . . I have tried to stand on the Constitution, but I am not afforded the rights another citizen may enjoy. I am forced to contend with communicating to the mass without words. I feel no man can represent another man because each man is different and has his own world, his own kingdom, his own reality. It is impossible to communicate one reality through another into another reality.

Despite Ball's favorable assessment of Manson, Keene was reluctant to appoint Manson as his own attorney:

> Mr. Manson, I am imploring you not to take this step; I am imploring you to either name your own attorney, or, if you are unable to do so, to permit the Court to name one for you. It is, in this Court's opinion, a sad and tragic mistake that you are making by taking this course of action, but I can't talk you out of it. . . . Mr. Manson, you are your own lawyer.[25]

Manson relished the powers afforded him as his own attorney and immediately went about the process of seeing how far he could take them. He demanded that every document pertaining to the case be photocopied and delivered to his jail cell. He conferred an astounding 147 times with outside attorneys. He arranged meetings with high-profile counterculture personalities who he thought might be sympathetic with his cause. Manson requested unlimited telephone privileges; he asked to be free to travel outside the prison. By the end of January Manson made his most outlandish request: He asked for the names, addresses, and telephone numbers of the prospective witnesses for the prosecution. The request was denied.

Manson Goes to Work

Although separated from the rest of his Family, Charles Manson continued to exert a great deal of control over them. Knowing that most of the evidence against him came from Susan Atkins, he sent Family members Squeaky Fromme and Sandra Good to visit Atkins in prison. Although one guard described the visits as sisterly, it was obvious to the prosecution that the girls were relaying messages from Manson to Atkins. As a result, Bugliosi was not surprised to hear that Atkins had made a formal request to talk to Manson. Legally, the meeting between Manson and Atkins could not be prevented. The hour-long reunion took place on March 6, 1970. According to observers, Atkins left the room smiling and giggling. Following the meeting, she fired her attorney, Richard Caballero, and replaced him with Daye Shinn, a man who had been meeting regularly with Manson. After meeting with Atkins, Shinn told the press that Atkins "will definitely deny everything she told the grand jury."[26]

"Outlandish" Motions

On March 6 Manson brought another unusual motion before Judge Keene. He asked that the "Deputy District Attorneys in charge of the trial be incarcerated for a period of time under the same circumstances that I have been subject to."[27] Judge Keene was not amused. Citing Manson's list of "outlandish" motions and numerous violations of the gag order, he announced, "Mr. Manson, your status, at this time, of acting as your own attorney is now vacated."[28] Keene appointed Charles Hollopeter as Manson's attorney.

Manson was furious. "You can kill me," he yelled, "but you can't give me an attorney! I won't take one!" Manson's parting words that day made all the papers: "There is no God in this courtroom!"[29] Manson continued to fight the judge's order. On March 19, after Hollopeter made two motions with which Manson disagreed, Manson tried to fire him and act as his own attorney. When Judge Keene denied his request, Manson responded by holding up a copy of the U.S. Constitution, crumpling it into a ball, and throwing it into a nearby wastebasket. Realizing that he could not act as his own attorney but furious at Hollopeter, Manson asked to be represented by attorney Ronald Hughes. Keene granted the request.

On April 13 Manson filed an affidavit of prejudice against Judge Keene, asking that the case be reassigned to another judge. Keene accepted Manson's request and turned the case over to Judge Charles H. Older. Manson continued to ask to act as his own attorney, but Older was no more sympathetic to Manson's request to represent himself than Keene had been.

Two weeks before the Tate-LaBianca murder trial was to begin, Manson asked the court to remove Hughes as his attorney and replace him with Irving Kanarek. Judge Older granted the substitution. Kanarek had a reputation as an "obstructionist" attorney—one who employs delay tactics to impede the progress of a trial. By continuously raising objections and speaking as long

IRVING KANAREK: "THE OBSTRUCTIONIST"

When it became clear to Charles Manson that he would not be able to act as his own attorney, he searched for an attorney who would mount a campaign of disruptive tactics and frivolous delays. One of Manson's advisers mentioned Irving Kanarek, an attorney legendary in Los Angeles for his obstructionist tactics. Defending a murder suspect in the so-called Onion Field murder case, Kanarek fought the court procedures to the point that after eighteen months the jury had not been selected and not a single witness had been called. By the second year of that trial, the district attorney chose to retire rather than continue with the trial.

Stories about Kanarek's idiosyncrasies abound. Kanarek had the unusual habit of wearing a new suit on the first day of a trial and continuing to wear the same suit every day until the case ended or the suit had to be discarded. He once lodged an objection that consisted of a single sentence made up of 148 words. He even objected when one witness stated his name for the record, claiming that witness's knowledge of his own name was hearsay evidence.

Manson defense attorney Irving Kanarek.

During the Manson Family trial, Kanarek objected almost continuously to Linda Kasabian's testimony. Moments after being warned by Judge Older not to raise any further objections, Kanarek objected to a statement by prosecutor Vincent Bugliosi. For defying his order, Judge Older found Kanarek in contempt of court and ordered him to spend a night in the county jail.

as possible when he did, Kanarek had once drawn out an ordinary robbery case for eighteen months.

Worried that Kanarek might drag out the Tate-LaBianca trial for months if not years, Bugliosi informed Older that the district attorney's office would not object to Manson acting as his own attorney. Older asked Manson if he was happy with his selection of Kanarek. "I thought I already explained that," Manson replied. "I would not be happy with anyone but myself. No man can represent me."[30] Nevertheless, Older was not convinced that Manson could adequately defend himself. "It would be a miscarriage of justice to permit you to represent yourself in a case having the complications this case has," Older said. The judge again asked Manson if he would affirm Kanarek as his attorney. "I am forced into a situation," Manson replied. "My second alternative is to cause you as much trouble as possible."[31] With that, Manson reluctantly affirmed Kanarek as his attorney.

The Trouble Begins

Manson had threatened to cause trouble, and he was true to his word. At his next appearance in court, on June 9, Manson turned his chair around and sat with his back to the judge. "The Court has shown me no respect, so I am going to show the Court the same thing,"[32] Manson declared. The next day the three female defendants shouted in unison, "If the court won't respect Mr. Manson's rights, they need not respect ours."[33] They too turned their chairs around in imitation of Manson. The defendants were removed, only to return on June 12 with more melodramatics.

Manson began the June 12 session with still another request to act as his own attorney. When Older refused to consider the matter, Manson extended his arms outward, dropped his head, and stood in the pose of a mock crucifixion. "You might as well crucify me now!"[34] he said. The three girls stood and did the same. After repeatedly calling for order, Older had the defendants removed from the courtroom. This time Manson was hostile. He fought the bailiffs until he was subdued and handcuffed.

When jury selection began on June 15, Manson was uncharacteristically sullen. After the first day, Manson, in a fit of petulance, ordered his attorney not to question the members of the jury pool. Throughout the jury selection, which took six weeks, Manson refused to let Kanarek say anything. During the process of selecting a jury, attorneys can probe potential jurors for possible biases that might affect their judgment of the facts. Attorneys are allowed to challenge, or disqualify, jurors who seem unable to judge the evidence fairly. By stopping his attorney from exercising this important right, Manson forfeited one of his best chances to influence the outcome of the trial. He allowed the prosecution to handpick a jury to its liking.

The Trial Begins

The jury was seated and Judge Older called the trial of Charles Manson, Susan Atkins, Patricia Krenwinkel, and Leslie Van Houten to order on Friday, July 24, 1970. Vincent Bugliosi and Aaron Stovitz sat at the prosecutor's table. The defendants and their lawyers sat at the defense table. Irving Kanarek represented Charles Manson, Daye Shinn represented Susan Atkins, Paul Fitzgerald represented Patricia Krenwinkel, and Ronald Hughes represented Leslie Van Houten.

As soon as the defendants entered the courtroom, it was clear that Manson was not going to confine his bizarre behavior to the pretrial proceedings. Manson appeared at the defendant's table with a bloody X carved in his forehead. Outside the courtroom, Family members handed out a statement from Manson explaining the X. It stated, in part,

I have X'd myself from your world. . . . I am not allowed to be a man in your society. I am considered inadequate and incompetent to speak or defend myself in your court. You have created the monster. I am not part of you, from you; nor do I condone your wars or your unjust attitudes towards things, animals and people.[35]

Ignoring Manson's theatrics, prosecutor Bugliosi began the trial by telling the jury in his opening statement that he would expose Charles Manson as the mastermind behind the Tate-LaBianca murders:

What kind of a diabolical mind would contemplate or conceive of these seven murders? What kind of mind would want to have seven human beings brutally murdered?

We expect the evidence at this trial to answer that question and show that defendant Charles Manson owned that diabolical mind.[36]

Bugliosi explained the Helter Skelter motive to the jury and described how Manson dominated his followers. He then began to introduce the evidence that tied all of the defendants to the Tate-LaBianca murders.

As a witness for the prosecution, Colonel Paul Tate identified the photograph of his dead daughter, Sharon Tate. Steven Parent's father, Wilfred Parent, was the second witness called. He wept as he identified the photograph of his slain son. Some jurors were moved to tears by the testimony of Tate and Parent.

After speaking with Manson, Susan Atkins replaced her lawyer with attorney Daye Shinn (pictured).

When the trial resumed on Monday, July 27, 1970, Linda Kasabian was scheduled to testify. The prosecution's star witness was escorted by eight armed guards as she made her way to the Hall of Justice. Despite all of the precautions, Manson Family member Sandra Good appeared in the corridor of the ninth-floor courtroom and confronted the witness. Good screamed at Kasabian, "You'll kill us all; you'll kill us all!"[37]

Despite the confrontation, Kasabian remained poised as she entered the courtroom. As she raised her hand to be sworn in, Irving Kanarek stood and shouted, "We object to this witness, Your Honor, on the grounds that she is incompetent and insane!"[38] Bugliosi immediately asked that Kanarek's remark be stricken from the record and that the judge find him in contempt of court for gross misconduct. Judge Older called for order. Older overruled the defense's objection and allowed the prosecution to begin questioning Kasabian.

Despite the attempt to intimidate her, Kasabian went ahead with her testimony. Led by Bugliosi's questions, the diminutive twenty-year-old began two days of the most chilling testimony ever heard in an American courtroom.

"Go with Tex and Do What He Tells You"

Kasabian had been on her own since the age of sixteen, living in at least four hippie communes across the country at various times. She joined Manson's commune at Spahn Ranch only a short time before the Tate-LaBianca killings. Although a newcomer to the Family, Kasabian was sent on Manson's murderous mission for the simple reason that she was the only Manson Family member with a valid driver's license.

Kasabian testified that she had dressed in dark clothes the night of August 8, then took her place behind the wheel of the Family's run-down 1959 Ford. Tex Watson got in the passenger side; Krenwinkel and Atkins got in the back. Kasabian thought she was taking the Family members on a "creepy crawly"—the term

Patricia Krenwinkel, Susan Atkins, and Leslie Van Houten (from left) often laughed and talked with the press on their way to the courtroom.

the Family used for a type of training mission in which they practiced sneaking into buildings undetected. Kasabian testified that Manson told her to "Go with Tex and do what he tells you to do."[39]

As Kasabian linked Manson to the killings, she momentarily glanced at her former lover and cult master. As their eyes met Manson smiled and slowly drew his index finger across his throat—a common gesture for execution or death. Kasabian as well as several jury members saw the ominous pantomime.

Ignoring the implied threat, Kasabian continued her testimony. She told how she and the other killers climbed the wall at 10050 Cielo Drive and dropped onto the lawn. Christmas lights, deliberately left hanging year-round by Sharon Tate, twinkled silently on the house in the distance. When a car came down the driveway toward the intruders, Tex Watson ordered the others to hide while he approached the vehicle. Kasabian said that she heard a young man's voice from the darkness and then four muffled shots. Watson then lead the group up to the house. He ordered Kasabian around back to find an open window or an unlocked door. Frightened by the shooting, Kasabian lied to Watson when she returned. Hoping Watson would call off the attack, she told him that there were no openings. Receiving this news, Watson simply forced open a window, then sent Kasabian back to the front of the house to keep watch. Kasabian told the jury what happened next: "I waited for a few minutes, and then all of a sudden I heard people screaming, saying 'No, please no!' It was just horrible . . . even my emotions cannot tell you how horrible it was."[40]

According to her account of the events, Kasabian repeatedly asked for the killing to stop:

> I wanted them to stop. I knew what they had done [to Steven Parent] and I knew they were killing these people. . . . A man was just coming out the door and he had blood all over his face. . . . We looked into each other's eyes for a minute, I don't know however long, and I said, "Oh God, I am so sorry. Please make it stop." And then he just fell to the ground into the bushes. And then Sadie came running out of the house, and I said, "Sadie, please make it stop!" And she said, "It's too late."[41]

To disrupt the damaging testimony, Kanarek objected continuously. On the first day alone Kanarek objected more than one hundred times. By the end of the week Kanarek and the other defense attorneys had objected almost nine hundred times. After repeatedly warning Kanarek about his tactics, Judge Older found him in contempt of court and ordered him to spend the night in jail.

Despite the constant interruptions, Kasabian went on to tell how the second night of murders unfolded at the LaBianca home. At one point Manson shouted to her, "You're telling lies!" Kasabian looked at him and answered, "No, I'm not Charlie. I'm telling the truth and you know it."[42] Kasabian had talked back to the person that *Rolling Stone* magazine had labeled "the Most Dangerous Man in the World."

After Kasabian's testimony was complete, the defense was allowed to cross-examine her. The cross-examination lasted a week, but Kasabian never wavered in her account. At the conclusion of Kasabian's testimony, courtroom reporter Theo Wilson commented,

> In ten days on the stand she has been a dramatic, remorseful, and reformed girl who never forgets to place the blame for seven violent murders right where the state wants it—on Charles (Messiah) Manson, the little man who wasn't there when any of the killings happened. Without Kasabian's testimony the state would've had almost no case at all.[43]

Bugliosi might have been speaking for everyone involved in the trial when he said, "If ever there was a star witness for the prosecution, Linda Kasabian was it."[44]

Manson understood how devastating Kasabian's testimony was to his case. As the evidence against him began to mount, Manson observed, "We did pretty good at the first of it. Then we kind of lost control when the testimony started."[45]

Chapter 5

Testimony and Tumult

As THE EVIDENCE PILED up against Charles Manson and his
followers, the self-styled guru began to behave even more
outrageously—shouting at witnesses, cursing at the judge, scuf-
fling with the bailiffs. This did not come as a surprise to Vincent
Bugliosi, who later observed: "By now I could see the pattern.
The more damaging the testimony, the more chance [that] Manson would create a disturbance, thereby assuring that he—and
not the evidence itself—would get the day's headlines."[46] Manson's outrageous behavior certainly did not help his case. The
prosecution portrayed him as an antisocial madman, and Manson
appeared all too willing to play the part.

Manson's attempts to disrupt the trial were held in check by
Judge Older, who did not hesitate to remove Manson, Atkins,
Krenwinkel, and Van Houten from the courtroom whenever they
defied his calls to order. Older had to be careful about removing
the defendants from the courtroom, however. The Sixth Amend-
ment of the U.S. Constitution guarantees every citizen the right
"to be confronted with the witnesses against him" and "to have
the Assistance of Counsel for his defence." If barring Manson
and his followers from the courtroom prevented them from hearing the evidence against them or from consulting with their attorneys while court was in session, their convictions could be
overturned on constitutional grounds. As a result, Older made
sure the defendants were present as often as possible.

Under Older's strong hand, Manson was unable to derail the
proceedings on his own. With help from the outside, however,
Manson managed to bring the trial to a standstill and nearly

Susan Atkins (seated) often followed the lead of Manson in court: If he folded his arms and turned his back on the judge, she would do the same.

caused a mistrial. The aid he received did not come from members of his Family who camped out on the steps of the courthouse. Instead, it came from the most unlikely of sources: the president of the United States.

"A Man Who Was Guilty"

At an appearance before a group of law enforcement officials in Denver, Colorado, President Richard Nixon strayed from his prepared remarks to comment on the Manson trial. Nixon believed that the media too often glamorized criminals and portrayed prosecutors as sinister. "I noted, for example, the coverage of the Charles Manson case when I was in Los Angeles, front page every day in the papers," Nixon began. "Here is a man who was guilty, directly or indirectly, of eight murders without reason. Here is a man, yet, who, as far as the [media] coverage was concerned, appeared to be rather a glamorous figure."[47]

The president's remark passed unnoticed by most members of the press corps, but one journalist who was at the luncheon, Paul Healy of the *New York Daily News*, realized that Nixon's statement was news. Although the Manson trial was still in progress, the president of the United States had declared the country's most notorious murder suspect to be guilty. The nation's chief executive had ignored the presumed innocence of a defendant. Healy immediately called his colleague in Los Angeles, Theo Wilson, who had been covering the Manson trial since it began. Wilson knew that in a trial like this, she had front-page news.

Even before *Air Force One* left Denver for its next destination, White House press secretary Ron Ziegler tried to smooth over his boss's gaffe. "The President inadvertently left out the word 'alleged' in his 'informal' remarks,"[48] said Ziegler. He then released a statement from the president:

> I have been informed that my comment in Denver regarding the Tate murder trial in Los Angeles may continue to be misunderstood despite the unequivocal statement made at the time by my press secretary. My remarks were in the context of my expression of a tendency on the part of some to glamorize those identified with a crime. The last thing I would want to do is prejudice the legal rights of any person, in any circumstances. To set the record straight, I do not know now and I did not intend to speculate as to whether the Tate defendants are guilty, in fact, or not. All the facts in the case have not yet been presented. The defendants should be presumed to be innocent at this stage of the trial.[49]

The press ignored Nixon's efforts to clarify his statement. Wilson skipped lunch in hopes of locating a member of the defense team for a response. She found defense attorney Ron Hughes and read him Nixon's statement. Hughes was livid. "Richard Nixon is a lawyer," said Hughes. "He should know better than that. I am dismayed that the President of the United States would violate a defendant's rights . . . and jeopardize a lengthy and expensive trial with such a thoughtless remark."[50]

"HERE IS A MAN WHO WAS GUILTY"

When President Richard Nixon spoke before a group of trial lawyers on August 3, 1970, he had no idea that his remarks would cause a national uproar and nearly wreck the nation's most sensational trial. The full text of his comments were carried in the *Los Angeles Times* on August 4, 1970.

Another point I would like to make is with regard to the responsibility of the American people, and also of those in the news media in this field. . . . The main concern that I have is the attitudes that are created among many of our younger people, and also perhaps older people as well, in which they tend to glorify and make heroes out of those who engage in criminal activities. This is not done intentionally by the press. It is not done intentionally by radio and television, I know. It is done perhaps because people want to read or see that kind of story.

I noted for example, the coverage of the Charles Manson case when I was in Los Angeles. . . . Here is a man who was guilty, directly or indirectly, of eight murders without reason. Here is a man, yet, who—as far as the coverage was concerned—appeared to be rather a glamorous figure, a glamorous figure to the young people whom he had brought into his operations. Another thing that was noted was the fact that two lawyers in the case . . . who were guilty of the most outrageous, contemptuous action in the courtroom, and who were ordered to jail overnight by the judge—seem to be more the oppressed, and the judge seemed to be the villain.

Let us understand, all judges are not heroes. All policemen are not heroes. And all those charged with crime are not guilty. But let us understand, too, that the system—the system in which we protect the rights of the innocent in which the guilty man receives a fair trial and gets the best possible defense—that system must be preserved.

The rest of the defense team agreed with Hughes. They moved to have the trial dismissed. Defense attorney Paul Fitzgerald said,

The fact that the President of the United States thinks that it is necessary to comment on the guilt or innocence of the defendants in this murder trial shows that the case has been prejudiced by pre-trial publicity to the point where we cannot get a fair trial. You have to realize that you can't deal with prejudice on such a massive scale. If the President of the United States says somebody is guilty, what recourse do you have?[51]

The jurors had been in the break room eating lunch when Nixon made his remarks, so they did not know about them. To make certain that the jury did not find out about these potentially prejudicial remarks, Older ordered that the windows of the buses carrying the jurors back to the hotel be covered so that there would be no possibility of any juror seeing a newspaper headline in a newsstand. The judge also ordered that the jurors, who usually watched television during the evenings, could not watch television that night or listen to the radio. Guards were placed at the hotels to enforce this rule. Wilson later recalled, "It may have been possible that the only twelve people in the whole country who hadn't seen some version of that headline were the jurors themselves."[52]

Manson Acts

The jury made it back to the courtroom the next day without having heard about the president's remark, but even these extraordinary precautions were not enough. When Susan Atkins's attorney, Daye Shinn, stood to address the court, Manson also stood. Without saying a word, he picked up a folded copy of the *Los Angeles Times*, faced the jury, and snapped the paper open in front of them. The headline was large enough to be read from across the room: "Manson Guilty, Nixon Declares." The courtroom was in an immediate uproar. The bailiffs grabbed Manson, wrested the paper from him, and whisked him away.

Kanarek immediately asked for a mistrial. He even went so far as to accuse the president of being involved in a conspiracy against his client. Older remained calm. To assess what effect, if any, the news had on the jury, Older questioned each juror separately about the incident.

Of the twelve jurors and six alternates, eleven had seen part or all of the headline. Those who had seen the headline had a variety of responses to it. "If the President did say something like that, then it was pretty stupid of him," said one woman. "No one does my thinking for me," said another. A third juror was unfazed: "I don't believe Mr. Nixon knows *anything* about it."[53] Older was satisfied that the objectivity of the jurors had not been compromised. The judge then turned to the issue of how Manson had gotten the newspaper in the first place. Older questioned the attorneys, the courtroom staff, and the bailiffs. Shinn confessed that Manson may have gotten the newspaper from his briefcase. Older held Shinn in contempt of court, and the attorney spent the weekend in jail.

Older denied the motions for a mistrial based on the headline incident, and bailiffs returned Manson to the courtroom. Bugliosi noticed that Manson was grinning as he entered the courtroom. "Charlie had made the big time," Bugliosi later observed. "It isn't every criminal who merits the attention of the President of the United States."[54]

Manson seemed to relish the moment. He released a statement mocking the president, who was the commander in chief of the armed forces fighting in the Vietnam War. "Here's this fellow Nixon, who's guilty—directly or indirectly—of hundreds of thousands of murders in Vietnam, and he's accusing me of eight murders,"[55] said Manson. When the trial resumed the next morning, Krenwinkel, Atkins, and Van Houten stood and shouted in one voice, "Your Honor, the President said we are guilty, so why go on with the trial?"[56] Older ordered the three defendants removed from the courtroom.

"Oh God!"

When the furor over Nixon's statement had subsided, the defense resumed the cross-examination of Linda Kasabian and calm returned to the courtroom. The quiet did not last long, however. Rather than trying to pick apart Kasabian's story fact by fact, Irving Kanarek decided to try to shock the witness into contradicting herself. Kanarek handed Kasabian a glossy color photograph of Sharon Tate taken after her death. "Mrs. Kasabian," said Manson's attorney, "I show you this picture." Kasabian was appalled by what she saw. "Oh God!"[57] she cried.

Linda Kasabian (foreground) leaves a Los Angeles courtroom. Her shock at seeing gruesome photos of the crime scene supported her contention that she was not present during the murders.

Kasabian began to weep and shake uncontrollably. Judge Older called for the court to recess.

When Kasabian was able to continue, Kanarek showed her more crime scene pictures. Kanarek's plan backfired. Kasabian never wavered in her account of the murders, and her shock at seeing the photographs seemed to confirm that she had not been in the house when the murders occurred. Her emotional response to the images suggested that she was sorry that the crimes had been committed.

Kanarek's brutal cross-examination continued for more than a week. Through it all Kasabian denied hurting any of the victims.

She also denied the charge that she was testifying against the others only to win immunity for herself. The defense accused her of being a liar, a drug addict, a witch, and a harlot. Speaking to reporters outside the court, attorney Paul Fitzgerald maligned Kasabian's testimony. "Anyone who has taken this much LSD over a prolonged period of time, cannot tell truth from reality,"[58] he said.

When the cross-examination was over, the prosecutor was allowed to ask a few more questions to clarify issues raised by the defense. Kasabian once again was completely frank. "You loved Charlie didn't you," Bugliosi asked Kasabian. "Yes, I did. I still do. But I believe he could take the truth and make a lie out of it."[59]

A Colorful Cowboy

Linda Kasabian's eyewitness account of the murders, along with the physical evidence, provided the jury with sufficient proof to convict Atkins, Krenwinkle, and Van Houten, but not Manson. Although Kasabian corroborated the Helter Skelter motive and Manson's domination of the group, she did not witness the conversation that took place between Tex Watson and Manson prior to the Tate murders. Although it was logical to conclude that Manson had ordered Watson to carry out the killings, Kasabian could not swear that he had. It was possible that Manson had told Watson to do something else and that Watson had decided to commit the murders on his own. To remove doubt about Manson's violent nature and his direct involvement in the murders, the prosecution called a witness named Juan Flynn to testify.

Flynn had worked for the owner of Spahn Ranch, George Spahn, for a number of years before the Manson Family moved in. Flynn described himself as a "part-time stuntman and full-time manure-shoveler."[60] Flynn testified that on several occasions Manson had tried to recruit him to become a member of his Family. Flynn said that he had been amused by the carefree lifestyle of the Family but had never considered joining the group. When the police raided the ranch on August 16, 1969, Flynn was taken into custody along with the rest of the family. Flynn immediately distanced himself from Manson and his followers and even agreed to testify against them.

Of all the witnesses for the prosecution, Bugliosi found Juan Flynn the most engaging and refreshing. Unlike the dozens of witnesses who were terrified by the idea of testifying against the alleged killers, Flynn seemed to relish the prospect of it. Most of the witnesses had to be subpoenaed to give their testimony; Flynn called Bugliosi's office and volunteered. Flynn's reasons were personal. His friend and coworker Donald "Shorty" Shea had been missing for months. Flynn was certain Manson was behind Shea's disappearance. After Flynn moved away from Spahn Ranch, he received threatening and abusive phone calls that he assumed came from Manson's followers. Flynn's reaction to the threats was to become even more determined to tell what he knew about the Family's activities.

"I'm the One Who's Doing All These Killings!"

Flynn was an even more credible witness than Linda Kasabian because, unlike Kasabian, Flynn was not seeking immunity for any wrongdoing. In addition, Flynn was talkative and colorful on the stand. Most importantly, Flynn had one credential that no other prosecution witness could claim: He had survived a murder threat by Manson himself. Bugliosi recalls Flynn's story:

> In questioning Juan, I established that the conversation had taken place in the kitchen at the Spahn Ranch, two to four days after news of the Tate murders broke on TV. Juan had just sat down to lunch when Manson came in and, with his right hand, brushed his left shoulder— apparently a signal that the others were to get out, since they immediately did. Aware that something was up, but not what, Juan started to eat. . . .
>
> Suddenly Manson grabbed Flynn by the hair, yanked his head back, and, putting a hunting knife to his throat, said . . . "Don't you know I'm the one who's doing all these killings!" . . . The razor-sharp blade still on Juan's throat, Manson asked, "Are you going to come with me or do I have to kill you?"

The diminutive Manson leaves court under guard.

Juan replied, "I'm eating right now, and I am right here, you know."[61]

Flynn's account of Manson's violent behavior and his admission of involvement in the Tate-LaBianca killings provided the prosecution with the link it needed to tie Manson to the murders. Flynn provided another important piece of testimony. He stated that the revolver used in the murders came from Spahn Ranch. He was sure it was the same gun because Manson had once aimed the .22 at him, shot, and missed. Kasabian had given the jury important eyewitness testimony, but the prosecution felt that Flynn's testimony cinched the case against Manson.

Outside the courtroom, the members of the Manson Family who were not in custody were carrying on a campaign of intimidation against witnesses and potential witnesses. On September 9

Barbara Hoyt, a Family member who agreed to testify for the prosecution, ate food that had been poisoned by another Family member. Hoyt recovered, but the threat to all witnesses was clear. On August 7 Randy Starr, another ranch hand at Spahn who was going to testify against Manson, died in an area hospital. The coroner performed an autopsy and ruled that the death was attributed to natural causes. Meanwhile Manson boasted that he had ordered a "hit" on Vincent Bugliosi.

"Somebody Should Cut Your Head Off"

As the trial continued, so did the outbursts from the defendants. The interruptions occurred so often that defendants spent much of the trial in a holding cell outside the courtroom, where they listened to the proceedings over a loudspeaker. When Bugliosi called Flynn as a witness, the outbursts grew to a crescendo. Bugliosi recalls,

> Several times while Flynn was on the stand, Older had to order Manson and the girls removed because of their outbursts. When it happened again, on October 2, Manson turned to the spectators and said: "Look at yourselves. Where are you going? You're going to destruction, that's where you're going." He then smiled a very odd little smile and added, "It's your Judgement Day, not mine." Again the girls parroted Manson, and Older ordered all removed.[62]

Although the outbursts had become common, no one anticipated the events that occurred when Sergeant Paul Whiteley of the Los Angeles County Sheriff's Office took the witness stand on October 5. After the officer had completed his testimony, Older asked the defense attorneys if they wanted to cross-examine the witness. Attorney Paul Fitzgerald declined the invitation, but Manson spoke up. *Los Angeles Times* reporter John Kendall, who was in the observers' gallery that day, explains what happened next:

> "Yes," Manson interjected. "May I examine him, your honor?"

MARTYR OR MADMAN?

The mainstream media portrayed Charles Manson as a disturbed criminal. A few members of the growing counterculture press, also known as the underground press, disputed this view. The underground newspaper *Tuesday's Child* chose Manson as its "Man of the Year." But *Rolling Stone* magazine, the leading counterculture publication of the era, labeled Manson "the World's Most Dangerous Man." In its January 4, 1970, issue, *Newsweek* magazine commented on some of the prevailing sentiments regarding Manson.

The underground press generally has assumed an uneasy ambivalence toward Manson, its rigid antiestablishment rhetoric sometimes making it appear Manson is on trial for his lifestyle rather than for murder. . . . Max Scherr, editor of the *Berkeley Barb* [says,] "It probably doesn't make much difference whether Manson is guilty or not. The minute the media created a drug-crazed hippie sticking forks in people's bellies, Charles Manson was doomed." Although Manson has not become a popular counterculture folk hero, there is a reluctance among street people to condemn him. For they see Manson as a martyr pitted against sadistic cops, money-hungry lawyers, bigoted and corrupt courts and sensation-seeking media.

Yet most longhairs take a dim view of Manson. No FREE MANSON buttons have blossomed, and the record of Manson's songs was a singular flop: of 2,000 produced, only 300 sold. "Manson is more than a villain. He is a leper," says the hip newspaper *Rolling Stone.*

"No, you may not," the judge said.

"Are you going to use this courtroom to kill me?" the defendant asked. . . . "Do you want me dead?" . . .

Older warned Manson that if he did not stop he would be removed from the courtroom. . . .

"Order me to be quiet while you kill me with your courtroom?" Manson asked. "Does that make sense? Am I supposed to lay here and just let you kill me? I am a human being. I am going to fight for my life, one way or another. You should let me do it with words."

Again the judge warned Manson that he would be removed, and the defendant continued:

"I will have you removed if you don't stop," yelled Manson. "I have a little system of my own!"[63]

With that, Manson snatched up a pencil, stepped onto the defense table, and from there leaped toward the judge. Manson fell short of the judge's bench and was tackled by three bailiffs. As they dragged him away, Manson screamed, "In the name of Christian justice somebody should cut your head off!"[64] Van Houten, Krenwinkel, and Atkins began chanting in unison and were removed from the courtroom.

When order was restored the defense attorneys called for a mistrial. "It isn't that easy, gentlemen," Older told them. "They are not going to profit from their own wrongdoing. Motion denied."[65]

Everyone in the courtroom was shocked by Manson's attack on Older, including the members of the jury who were to decide the defendant's fate. Through his actions, Manson had revealed that he was not the peace-loving hippie he had claimed to be. As Bugliosi later commented, "All masks had been dropped. They'd seen the real face of Charles Manson."[66]

On November 16, 1970, after twenty-two weeks of testimony, the prosecution rested their case against Charles Manson and his three female followers. Most legal analysts agreed that the prosecution had done a creditable job. But no one could be certain of the chances of a conviction until the defense had presented its case.

Chapter 6

The Jury Decides

B Y ITS FOURTH MONTH, the Manson Family trial had already become one of the longest and costliest criminal trials in California history. Many observers considered it the strangest trial as well. Before the jury would be asked for its decision, the case would take even more unusual twists and turns.

The biggest surprise occurred on Thursday, November 19, 1970, three days after the prosecution had rested its case. After sitting through twenty-two weeks of testimony, the defense finally was allowed to respond to the evidence. As the trial resumed, Judge Older took his seat behind the bench, greeted the courtroom, and told the defense to call its first witness. Paul Fitzgerald, head counsel for the defense, stood. "Thank you, your Honor," he said. "The defendants rest."[67] The courtroom was still. The only sound was Fitzgerald sliding his chair back into place at the defense table.

Under a law known as California Statute 1118, the defense is not obligated to present any case at all if it believes that the state has failed to prove guilt. By resting, Fitzgerald was suggesting that the prosecution had raised suspicions about the defendants but had failed to prove the suspicions were warranted.

The jury looked blankly at the judge for an explanation, but Older himself looked stunned. Someone in the courtroom gasped. The reporters rushed out of the room with the breaking news. The eerie silence was soon broken by a furious debate at the defense table. Krenwinkel, Van Houten, and Atkins stood and demanded to be heard. They wanted to testify, they said. Older called for order and then directed the attorneys to meet

him in his chambers for a conference. Behind closed doors,
Fitzgerald admitted to the judge
that the defense team was not
united. He explained that Krenwinkel, Van Houten, and Atkins
were planning to put all the
blame on themselves in an attempt to exonerate Manson. The
attorneys for the female defendants were opposed to their
clients' plan, Fitzgerald explained. The defense had rested
to avert the possibility that the
girls would take the stand and
incriminate themselves.

Older was forced to rule on
the unusual situation. Would it

*Attorney Paul Fitzgerald wanted
none of the accused to testify.*

serve justice to allow the defen-
dants to take the stand against the advice of their counsel and
make self-incriminating statements? Once back in the courtroom, Older warned Krenwinkel, Van Houten, and Atkins that
they were placing themselves in jeopardy by volunteering to testify. The women nevertheless insisted that they be allowed to
tell their story. Reluctantly, Older ruled in favor of the defendants. "The accused's right to testify is paramount,"[68] he said.

Ronald Hughes, attorney for Leslie Van Houten, was especially opposed to the defendants' plan. Because his client was
charged only in the LaBianca murders, Hughes believed that
she had the best chance to be found not guilty, and therefore
had the most to lose by testifying. "I refuse to take part in any
proceeding where I am forced to push my client out the window,"[69] he declared.

Manson Speaks

Shortly after Older had ruled that Van Houten, Krenwinkel, and
Atkins could testify, the bizarre trial took yet another twist:

Manson asked to testify. The judge said that he would allow Manson to make a statement, but not in the presence of the jury. After the jury left the courtroom, Manson was sworn in and took the stand. The defendant spoke for nearly two hours. Bugliosi found Manson's soliloquy mesmerizing. "He rambled, digressed, he repeated himself, but there was something hypnotic about the whole performance," Bugliosi recalls. "In his own strange way he was trying to weave the spell, not unlike the ones he had cast over his impressionable followers."[70] Manson stated, in part,

There has been a lot of charges and a lot of things said about me and brought against me and brought against the co-defendants in this case, of which a lot could be cleared up and clarified to where everyone could understand exactly what the family was supposed to have been.

These children that come at you with knives, they are your children. You taught them. I didn't teach them.

In the absence of the jury Manson was allowed to make a two-hour statement before the court.

MANSON TESTIFIES

On November 20, 1970, Charles Manson took the stand as a witness at his own trial. With the jury out of the room, Manson gave a rambling account of his background and his view of the society that sat in judgment of him. Manson's complete statement appears as an appendix in the book *Taming the Beast* by Edward George and Dary Matera.

These children that come at you with knives, they are your children. You taught them. I didn't teach them. I just tried to help them stand up. Most of the people at the ranch that you call The Family were just people that you did not want, people that were alongside the road, that their parents had kicked them out or they did not want to go to Juvenile Hall, so I did the best I could and I took them up on my garbage dump and I told them this, that in love there is no wrong. . . .

I have killed no one and I have ordered no one to be killed. I may have implied on several occasions to several different people that I may have been Jesus Christ, but I haven't decided yet what I am or who I am. I was given a name and a number and I was put in a cell, and I have lived in a cell with a name and a number. I don't know who I am. I am whoever you make me, but what you want is a fiend; you want a sadistic fiend because that is what you are. You only reflect on me what you are inside of yourselves. . . .

I live in my world, and I am my own king in my world, whether it be a garbage dump or if it be in the desert or wherever it be. I am my own human being. You may restrain my body . . . but I am still me and you can't take that. . . . I haven't got any guilt about anything because I have never been able to say any wrong. I never found any wrong. I looked at wrong, and it is all relative. . . .

I look at the jury and they won't look at me. . . . They are afraid of me. And do you know why they are afraid of me? Because of the newspapers. You projected fear. You made me a monster and I have to live with that the rest of my life because I cannot fight this case. If I could fight this case and I could present this case, I would take that monster back and I would take that fear back. Then you could find something else to put your fear on, because it's all your fear.

You look for something to project it on and you pick a little old scroungy nobody who eats out of a garbage can, that nobody wants, that was kicked out of the penitentiary, that has been dragged through every hellhole you can think of, and you drag him up and put him into a courtroom. You expect to break me? Impossible! You broke me years ago. You killed me years ago. I have reflected your society in yourselves, right back at yourselves.

I just tried to help them stand up. Most of the people at the ranch that you call The Family were just people that you did not want, people that were alongside the road, that their parents had kicked them out or they did not want to go to Juvenile Hall, so I did the best I could and I took them up on my garbage dump and I told them this that in love there is no wrong. . . .

I have killed no one and I have ordered no one to be killed. I may have implied on several occasions to several different people that I may have been Jesus Christ, but I haven't decided yet what I am or who I am. I was given a name and a number and I was put in a cell, and I have lived in a cell with a name and a number. I don't know who I am. I am whoever you make me, but what you want is a fiend; you want a sadistic fiend because that is what you are. You only reflect on me what you are inside of yourselves. . . .

You see, you can send me to the penitentiary, it's not a big thing. I've been there all my life anyway. But what about your children? These are just a few, there is many, many more coming right at you.[71]

Manson seemed satisfied with his performance. When he concluded, Judge Older asked him if he wanted to testify in front of the jury. "I've already relieved all the pressure I have," said Manson. When he returned to the defense table, Manson told his three fellow defendants, "You don't have to testify now."[72]

After twenty-three weeks, the testimony in the Tate-LaBianca trial was complete. Older ordered a ten-day recess in the trial to give attorneys time to prepare their closing arguments. During the break, the trial took one of the strangest turns of all.

Missing

When court resumed on Monday, November 30, Leslie Van Houten's attorney, Ron Hughes, was not in his chair. Hughes had told his friends that he was going to take a short vacation during the court recess, during which he would work on his presentation

—the first closing argument he had ever given in a felony case. After waiting fifteen minutes, Older, who had once found Irving Kanarek in contempt of court for being seven minutes late to court, was visibly upset. An hour passed, but Hughes had still not arrived. Older recessed the court once again. When the court failed to hear from Hughes again the next day, Older suspended the trial. Defense attorney Paul Fitzgerald told reporters, "I think Ron is dead."[73]

THE DEATH OF RON HUGHES

The disappearance of Ron Hughes, the attorney for Leslie Van Houten, caused the longest single delay in the trial and resulted in a great amount of speculation in the media. Thirty-year-old Hughes originally came onto the case as Manson's attorney. Manson felt an affinity toward Hughes, who was familiar with the counterculture and was therefore able to speak the language of the younger generation. With his casual dress, his full beard and longer hair, his appearance had more in common with the young defendants than with the other attorneys. In his pretrial meetings with Manson, Hughes gave the impression that he was willing to do Manson's bidding in the courtroom.

This willingness changed, however, when Hughes was reassigned as Van Houten's attorney. Late in the trial he openly opposed Manson's strategy of having Van Houten and the other female defendants claim sole responsibility for the murders. That stance may have cost Hughes his life. Contemporary press reports were split on the issue; even decades later knowledgeable opinions are divided on the cause of Hughes's death. When his body was found, it had been underwater for weeks. The condition of the corpse made it impossible for the coroner to rule whether death was caused by drowning or by other means.

Defense attorney Ron Hughes.

Vincent Bugliosi has stated that the Manson Family has secretly claimed responsibility for Hughes's death, but unless a former Family member comes forth with either details or a confession, it is likely the mystery of Hughes's death will remain unresolved.

Fitzgerald turned out to be correct, although no one knew it until Hughes's body was found fifteen weeks later. Fishermen in the Sespe River, near where Hughes liked to hike, made the grisly discovery. An autopsy was performed, but the corpse, which had been trapped underwater, was so badly decomposed that coroners were unable to determine the cause of death. Meanwhile, with one attorney missing, security was tightened for the judge and all of the members of the prosecution team.

With Hughes missing, Older assigned Maxwell Keith as replacement attorney for Van Houten. Keith asked Older for a three-week suspension of the trial so that he could review the case thoroughly. Older granted Keith's request.

Keith made it clear that he would do his best to represent Van Houten regardless of what Manson thought of his strategy. As a result, Manson was openly hostile toward the new attorney. On December 3 Manson complained to the court that the defense attorneys had no right to rest the case. Manson wanted the entire defense team dismissed. He had prepared his own line of defense, Manson said, and had more than twenty witnesses waiting to speak on his behalf. Older would have none of it. He denied Manson's request and set a date for the resumption of the trial.

Chaos in the Courtroom

The trial resumed on December 21, still without word about the whereabouts of Ron Hughes. Manson began the day by throwing paper clips at the judge. The three female defendants shouted at the judge, accusing him of "doing away with Hughes."[74] Older ordered all of the defendants to be removed from the courtroom. On the way out, Susan Atkins scuffled with the bailiffs as she lunged for a knife that lay on the evidence table.

It took three days for the prosecution to present its summary of the evidence to the jury. Vincent Bugliosi and his colleagues pointed out that in eighteen days of testimony Linda Kasabian gave no conflicting statements. In addition, the prosecution outlined the nearly three hundred occasions mentioned on the witness stand that pointed to Charles Manson's complete domination of his Family.

As the prosecution continued with its summation, Manson decided not to return to court. He chose instead to remain in a holding cell where he could listen to the proceedings but not be seen. His antics continued, however. He offered a bailiff a bribe in exchange for helping him escape. Unsuccessful, Manson tried to smuggle a hacksaw blade into his cell, but the guards stopped him. Outside the court, the Family members who had been keeping silent vigil became more and more vocal, challenging passersby and shouting threats into press cameras.

Even without Manson in the courtroom, the disruptions continued. During the prosecution's summation the female defendants caused a disturbance, and Older ordered them removed. As she was being escorted out, Atkins kicked a female deputy and grabbed Bugliosi's notes. Once again bailiffs grabbed Atkins and restrained her. Weary of the defendants' behavior, Older barred the defendants from appearing in court for the remainder of the trial. The judge commented, "I don't think any American court is required to subject itself to this kind of nonsense day after day when it is perfectly obvious that the defendants are using it to stage some kind of performance."[75]

Final Arguments

With the defendants banished to holding cells, Irving Kanarek took the floor to present his final argument to the jury. Kanarek finally offered a theory of what had happened. According to Kanarek, Tex Watson and Linda Kasabian, who had been lovers, were responsible for the murders. It was, he said, a case of "Love of a girl for a boy." Manson, Kanarek argued, was being persecuted for his anti-establishment views. "Now the people who brought these charges, they want to get Charles Manson, for some ungodly reason, which I think is related to Manson's life style,"[76] Kanarek declared.

Kanarek's argument was simple, but his presentation of it was not. The defense attorney stretched his argument out for seven full days. Finally, Judge Older reprimanded him:

> You are abusing your right to argue just as you have abused practically every other right you have in this case.

. . . There is a point, Mr. Kanarek, at which argument is no longer argument, but filibuster. . . . I have come to the regretful conclusion during the course of the trial that Mr. Kanarek appears to be totally without scruples, ethics, and professional responsibility . . . and I want the record to clearly reflect that.[77]

Even Manson, who was listening from his holding cell, grew impatient with his attorney's tactics. "Why don't you just sit down?" Manson yelled. "You're just making things worse."[78] When Kanarek concluded, the transcript of his remarks took up 1,182 pages.

On January 13, 1971, Bugliosi began his closing argument. In criminal trials, the prosecution has the last word before the jury deliberates. For three days Bugliosi reviewed the evidence, especially the testimony of Linda Kasabian. On January 15, exactly seven months after the trial had started, Bugliosi concluded his summation. His final words rang with a passionate plea for justice:

On the hot summer night of August the eighth, 1969, Charles Manson . . . sent out from the fires of hell at Spahn Ranch three heartless, bloodthirsty robots and—unfortunately for him—one human being, the little hippie girl Linda Kasabian.

The photographs of the victims show how very well Watson, Atkins, and Krenwinkel carried out their master Charles Manson's mission of murder. . . .

What resulted was perhaps the most inhuman, nightmarish, horror-filled hour of savage murder and human slaughter in the recorded annals of crime. . . .

Based on the evidence that came from the witness stand, not only isn't there any reasonable doubt of their guilt, which is our only burden, there is absolutely no doubt whatsoever of their guilt. . . .

Ladies and gentlemen of the jury, Sharon Tate . . . Abigail Folger . . . Voytek Frykowski . . . Jay Sebring . . . Steven

Parent . . . Leno LaBianca . . . Rosemary LaBianca . . . are not here with us now in the courtroom, *but from their graves they cry out for justice.* Justice can only be served by coming back to this courtroom with a verdict of guilty.[79]

After a recess, Judge Older gave the jury its instructions. At 3:20 in the afternoon, the jury filed out of the courtroom to deliberate.

The Verdicts

For two days there was no word from the jury or any indication of progress. On the third day of deliberations, the jurors asked for a copy of the Beatles' *White Album* to be played for them. They also

The Manson guilty verdict warranted a special edition of the Los Angeles Times.

reviewed some of Susan Atkins's letters to her former cell mates. The deliberations continued for several more days. The press began to speculate that the jury was deadlocked and would not be able to come to a unanimous decision. Finally, after nine days of deliberations, the jury informed the judge that they had come to a verdict.

The jury returned to the courtroom. It took the jury foreman thirty-eight minutes to read the verdicts for all four defendants on each count of murder and conspiracy to commit murder. The jury found Manson, Atkins, Krenwinkel, and Van Houten guilty of all charges.

The defendants showed little reaction as the verdicts were read. Afterward, as they were led away, Manson pointed at Older and yelled, "We still are not allowed to put on a defense? You won't outlive that, old man."[80]

Life or Death?

After the verdicts were handed down, the Manson Family trial began its penalty phase. In California courts there are two phases of a trial. In the first phase the jury must decide if the defendants are guilty of the charges. If guilt is proven, the trial enters a second phase—the penalty phase. During this phase the jury decides what punishment the defendants will receive. Vincent Bugliosi later explained the purpose of the penalty phase in the Tate-LaBianca case: "During the penalty trial the sole issue for the jury to decide was whether the defendants should receive life imprisonment or the death penalty. Considerations like mitigating circumstances, background, remorse, and the possibility of rehabilitation were therefore now relevant."[81]

The penalty phase is normally brief, but under Manson's direction, the defense called a large number of witnesses to testify on the defendants' behalf. Over the course of the next two months, a dozen Family members took the witness stand. All denied that Manson had any influence over their lives. Several witnesses took responsibility for ordering the murders. Atkins took the stand and denounced the Helter Skelter motive as ridiculous. She suggested that the Tate-LaBianca murders were carried out as copycat crimes to confuse the investigation of Gary

Hinman's murder. The defense then called doctors to the stand to testify that LSD had rendered the defendants incapable of telling right from wrong.

The parents of the female defendants took the stand and gave heartfelt testimony about their daughters. Patricia Krenwinkel's father, Joseph, described his daughter as an "exceedingly normal child, very obedient."[82] Krenwinkel's mother, Dorothy, stated that her daughter "would rather hurt herself than harm any living thing." When asked if she loved her daughter, Dorothy Krenwinkel answered, "I did love my daughter; I will always love my daughter; and no one will ever convince me that she did anything terrible or horrible."[83] Leslie Van Houten's mother, Jane, echoed those sentiments. When Maxwell Keith, who had replaced the missing Ronald Hughes as Van Houten's attorney, asked Jane Van Houten, "How do you feel about your daughter now?" she answered, "I love Leslie very much." "As much as you always have?" Keith asked. "More,"[84] she replied.

With their heads shaved, Van Houten, Atkins, and Krenwinkel (from left) leave the court after the death penalty verdict.

The Death Penalty

After eight weeks of testimony in the penalty phase, the jurors began deliberations. On March 29, 1971, the jury returned. The jurors were not willing to show any more mercy than the killers had shown their victims. They said, "We the jury in the above-entitled action, having found the defendant[s] guilty of murder in the first degree . . . do fix the penalty of death."[85]

As the defendants were led away, each of the condemned killers yelled at the jury. "You have just judged yourselves!" shouted Krenwinkel. "Your whole system is a game! You blind, stupid people! Your own children will turn against you!" screamed Van Houten. "You'd best lock your doors and watch your own kids," Atkins chimed in. Turning to Judge Older, Atkins added, "You are removing yourselves from the face of the earth, you old fool!"[86]

After nine and a half months, the Tate-LaBianca trial was over. The jury had been sequestered for 225 days. The trial transcripts took up 31,716 typed pages. Every attorney on both sides of the case had been cited or threatened with contempt of court. One lawyer was dead.

The state of California faced an unusual problem at the conclusion of the Manson trial. The state did not have a facility to hold women awaiting execution. Atkins, Krenwinkel, and Van Houten would have to wait for the Department of Corrections to build a death row cell block for women, where they would live until they were executed.

A few months after the Manson trial concluded, Tex Watson was tried for his role in the murders. He also was found guilty and was sentenced to death. He joined his accomplices on death row to await his execution day—a day that, in another unusual twist, would never come for Watson or any of the Manson Family killers.

Epilogue

The Aftermath of Madness

A S CHARLES MANSON AND his accomplices waited to die in San Quentin prison's gas chamber, they received unexpected news. Opponents of capital punishment had appealed to the California Supreme Court to strike down death penalty laws as unconstitutional. On February 18, 1972, the California Supreme Court did just that. In *People v. Anderson*, Justice C.J. Wright wrote for the majority:

> We have concluded that capital punishment is impermissibly cruel. It degrades and dehumanizes all who participate in its processes. It is unnecessary to any legitimate goal of the state and is incompatible with the dignity of man and the judicial process. Our conclusion that the death penalty may no longer be exacted in California consistently with article I, section 6, of our Constitution is not grounded in sympathy for those who would commit crimes of violence, but in concern for the society that diminishes itself whenever it takes the life of one of its members.[87]

The ruling meant that anyone sentenced to death under the existing laws would automatically have their sentences commuted to life in prison. In 1976 the state reinstated the death penalty, but the new laws could not be applied to earlier cases. Manson and his followers would live, and they would even have the opportunity to be paroled.

Leslie Van Houten testifies at her thirteenth parole hearing in 2000.

Model Prisoners

In the three decades since the Tate-LaBianca murders, all of Manson's fellow defendants have renounced their former guru. Patricia Krenwinkel and Leslie Van Houten have been deemed model prisoners at Frontera State Prison. Both have earned college degrees. Van Houten was granted a retrial of her original conviction in 1976 due to matters arising from the death of Ronald Hughes, and she was convicted a second time. Each of the women has been denied parole almost twenty times. However, some experts believe that it is possible that the two may eventually be released.

Susan Atkins and Charles "Tex" Watson have both claimed to have had religious conversions during their time in prison, and both have published accounts of their lives. Watson married in 1979 and has fathered four children. Atkins married in 1987. Dozens of parole attempts have been denied for the two; some parole board members have expressed skepticism over their claims to having been reformed.

The Family Lives On

The five members of the Manson Family convicted of killing Sharon Tate and the other victims made up only a fraction of Manson's following. Many others have been arrested and imprisoned in the years following the Tate-LaBianca murders. Eight members were involved in a violent shoot-out with police while attempting to steal guns and ammunition from a Southern California sporting goods store. A theft of hand grenades from a California army base was later linked to an aborted plan to break Manson out of prison. Others were convicted in the murder of Donald "Shorty" Shea, a wrangler at Spahn Ranch. Sandra Good served ten years for sending death threats to heads of industry

Family member Sandra Good sent death threats to heads of industry whom she considered enemies of the environment.

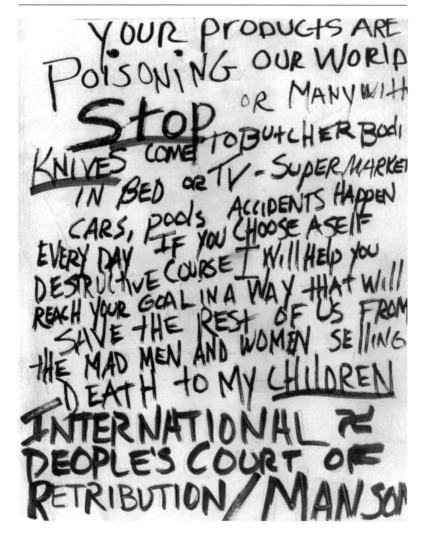

whom she considered enemies of the environment. Family members Bruce Davis and Nancy Pitman pled guilty to the murders of two college students who may have had information about Ron Hughes's disappearance. Davis is also suspected in the suspicious death of Good's estranged husband and in the series of unsolved murders known in California as the Zodiac Killings. In 1975 Lynette "Squeaky" Fromme attempted to assassinate President Gerald Ford and was sent to prison for life.

Charles Manson receives more mail than any incarcerated person in history. During most of his time as an inmate in California prisons he has been separated from the general prison population because of disciplinary infractions or at his own request. Manson has often feared for his life in prison. These fears were not groundless. Manson suffered severe burns when an inmate, seeking notoriety, doused Manson with paint thinner and set him ablaze. Although Manson is entitled to periodic parole hearings, he scoffs at the proceedings, once sending money from the board game Monopoly to the parole board members as a "bribe." Nuel Emmons, a former prison mate of Manson's, who spent hundreds of hours interviewing Manson while collaborating on a book, believes that Manson is doomed by his own infamy:

> He has created a larger than life image of himself. The majority of visitors and visitor requests that he has are strangers. Mothers want him to bless their babies. He has offers in the mail for marriage. A startling number of the letters contain offers to commit murder for him. Now he is held hostage by that. He will never be released.[88]

The case of Charles Manson and the Tate-LaBianca murders remains unique in American crime. Other mass murderers have taken more lives than Charles Manson did, but all of them did the killing themselves. Manson convinced others to kill for him. By inciting a small cell of followers to kill for a cause, Manson established himself as a kind of terrorist. He believed that the horrible nature of his crimes would frighten the public and lead to the breakdown of society—a common terrorist goal.

The enigmatic Manson smiles during a parole hearing in 1986.

Writer Theo Wilson believes that the Tate-LaBianca case will linger in the national memory as long as America has a sense of the horrible and a sense of conscience: "The Manson case, to this day, remains one of the most chilling in crime history. And as Charlie predicted, to the world he has remained a monster. Even people who were not yet born when the murders took place know the name Charles Manson and shudder."[89]

Notes

Introduction: The Killer Cult

1. Steven Roberts, "Charles Manson: One Man's Family," *New York Times Magazine*, January 4, 1970, p. 10.
2. Quoted in Vincent Bugliosi with Curt Gentry, *Helter Skelter: The True Story of the Manson Murders*, rev. ed., New York: W. W. Norton, 1994, p. 142.
3. Quoted in Bugliosi and Gentry, *Helter Skelter*, p. 141.

Chapter 1: Horror in Hollywood

4. Quoted in *Time*, "Nothing But Bodies," August 15, 1969, p. 24.
5. Quoted in Bugliosi and Gentry, *Helter Skelter*, p. 41.
6. John Phillips and Jim Jerome, *Papa John*. New York: Doubleday, 1986, p. 226.
7. Quoted in Bugliosi and Gentry, *Helter Skelter*, p. 45.
8. Quoted in Bugliosi and Gentry, *Helter Skelter*, p. 33.

Chapter 2: Confession and Capture

9. Susan Atkins, *Child of Satan, Child of God*. Plainfield, NJ: Logos International, 1977, p. 23.
10. Atkins, *Child of Satan, Child of God*, p. 48.
11. Quoted in Los Angeles Police Department, interrogation of Virginia Graham, 1969.
12. Quoted in Los Angeles Police Department, interrogation of Graham.
13. Quoted in Los Angeles Police Department, interrogation of Graham.
14. Quoted in the transcript of Los Angeles Police Department, interrogation of Ronnie Howard, 1969.
15. Bugliosi and Gentry, *Helter Skelter*, p. 119.

Chapter 3: The Case Against the Manson Family

16. Bugliosi and Gentry, *Helter Skelter*, p. 305.
17. Quoted in CBS News/A&E Network, *The Twentieth Century*, vol. 3, A&E Home Video, 1994, videocassette.

18. Quoted in Bugliosi and Gentry, *Helter Skelter,* p. 162.
19. Bugliosi and Gentry, *Helter Skelter,* p. 213.
20. *People v. Manson et al.,* trial transcript, January 1970.
21. Bugliosi and Gentry, *Helter Skelter,* p. 218.

Chapter 4: A Bizarre Defense

22. Quoted in John Kendall, "Manson Asks for 'Voice,'" *Los Angeles Times,* December 18, 1969, p. 2.
23. Quoted in John Kendall, "Ball Reports to Judge," *Los Angeles Times,* December 25, 1969, p. 1.
24. Bugliosi and Gentry, *Helter Skelter,* p. 201.
25. *People v. Manson et al.,* trial transcript, December 24, 1970.
26. Quoted in Bugliosi and Gentry, *Helter Skelter,* p. 266.
27. *People v. Manson et al.,* trial transcript, March 6, 1970.
28. *People v. Manson et al.,* trial transcript, March 6, 1970.
29. Quoted in John Kendall, "Manson Loses Pro Per," *Los Angeles Times,* March 6, 1970, p. 2.
30. Quoted in Bugliosi and Gentry, *Helter Skelter,* p. 296.
31. Quoted in Bugliosi and Gentry, *Helter Skelter,* p. 297.
32. Quoted in Bugliosi and Gentry, *Helter Skelter,* p. 297.
33. *People v. Manson et al.,* trial transcript, June 9, 1970.
34. *People v. Manson et al.,* trial transcript, June 12, 1970.
35. *Los Angeles Free Press,* "News in Brief: Manson's 'X' Statement," July 31–August 6, 1970, p. 2.
36. Bugliosi and Gentry, *Helter Skelter,* p. 311.
37. Quoted in Bugliosi and Gentry, *Helter Skelter,* p. 317.
38. Quoted in John Kendall "Mrs. Kasabian's Testimony Met by 50 Defense Objections," *Los Angeles Times,* July 28, 1970, p. 20.
39. Quoted in Jess Bravin, *Squeaky: The Life and Times of Lynette Alice Fromme,* New York: St. Martin's Press, 1997, p. 100.
40. Quoted in Kendall, "Witness Begins Story," *Los Angeles Times,* July 27, 1970, p. 18.
41. Quoted in Kendall, "Witness Begins Story," p. 18.
42. Quoted in Kendall, "Linda Kasabian Testifies She Loved Manson as the 'Messiah,'" *Los Angeles Times,* August 6, 1970, p. 17.
43. Theo Wilson, *Headline Justice.* New York: Thunder's Mouth, 1996, p. 171.

44. Bugliosi and Gentry, *Helter Skelter*, p. 332.
45. Quoted in Bugliosi and Gentry, *Helter Skelter*, p. 459.

Chapter 5: Testimony and Tumult

46. Bugliosi and Gentry, *Helter Skelter*, p. 368.
47. Quoted in "Text of Nixon Remarks on Press and Manson," *Los Angeles Times*, August 4, 1970, p. 10.
48. White House press release, August 4, 1970.
49. White House press release, August 4, 1970.
50. Quoted in Wilson, *Headline Justice*, p. 174.
51. Quoted in CBS News/A&E Network, *The Twentieth Century*.
52. Wilson, *Headline Justice*, p. 175.
53. Quoted in Bugliosi and Gentry, *Helter Skelter*, p. 327.
54. Bugliosi and Gentry, *Helter Skelter*, p. 325.
55. Quoted in *Los Angeles Free Press*, "Manson's 'Nixon' Statement," August 10, 1970, p. 2.
56. Quoted in Bugliosi and Gentry, *Helter Skelter*, p. 327.
57. Quoted in Bugliosi and Gentry, *Helter Skelter*, p. 329.
58. Quoted in CBS News/A&E Network, *The Twentieth Century*.
59. *People v. Manson et al.*, trial transcript, August 18, 1970.
60. *People v. Manson et al.*, trial transcript, September 27, 1970.
61. Quoted in Bugliosi and Gentry, *Helter Skelter*, pp. 333–34.
62. Bugliosi and Gentry, *Helter Skelter*, p. 368.
63. John Kendall, "Manson Attacks Judge," *Los Angeles Times*, October 6, 1970, p. 2.
64. Quoted in Kendall, "Manson Attacks Judge," p. 2.
65. *People v. Manson et al.*, trial transcript, October 5, 1970.
66. Bugliosi and Gentry, *Helter Skelter*, p. 370.

Chapter 6: The Jury Decides

67. Quoted in Bugliosi and Gentry, *Helter Skelter*, p. 383.
68. *People v. Manson et al.*, trial transcript, November 19, 1970.
69. Quoted in Bugliosi and Gentry, *Helter Skelter*, p. 387.
70. Bugliosi and Gentry, *Helter Skelter*, p. 388.
71. *People v. Manson et al.*, trial transcript, December 20, 1970.
72. Quoted in Bugliosi and Gentry, *Helter Skelter*, p. 392.
73. Quoted in Bugliosi and Gentry, *Helter Skelter*, p. 394.

74. Quoted in Bugliosi and Gentry, *Helter Skelter*, p. 397.
75. Quoted in Bugliosi and Gentry, *Helter Skelter*, p. 399.
76. Quoted in Bugliosi and Gentry, *Helter Skelter*, p. 402.
77. *People v. Manson et al.*, trial transcript, January 7, 1970.
78. Quoted in Bugliosi and Gentry, *Helter Skelter*, p. 403.
79. Bugliosi and Gentry, *Helter Skelter*, p. 408–409.
80. Quoted in Bugliosi and Gentry, *Helter Skelter*, p. 413.
81. Bugliosi and Gentry, *Helter Skelter*, p. 417.
82. Quoted in Bugliosi and Gentry, *Helter Skelter*, p. 417.
83. Quoted in Bugliosi and Gentry, *Helter Skelter*, p. 418.
84. Quoted in Bugliosi and Gentry, *Helter Skelter*, p. 419.
85. *People v. Manson et al.*, trial transcript, March 29, 1971.
86. Quoted in John Kendall, "Manson, Three Girls Receive Death Penalty," *Los Angeles Times*, March 30, 1971, p. 3.

Epilogue: The Aftermath of Madness

87. Findlaw, People v. Anderson, 6cal. 3d628. http://login.findlaw. com/scripts/callaw?dest=ca/cal3d/6/628.html.
88. The Manson Murders, www. mansonmurders.com.
89. Wilson, *Headline Justice*, p. 194.

Timeline

March 21, 1967
Charles Manson is released from Terminal Island Penitentiary after a ten-year term.

July 31, 1969
Gary Hinman is murdered by Bobby Beausoleil on orders from Manson.

August 6, 1969
Beausoleil is arrested in Hinman's car.

August 8, 1969
Sharon Tate, Wojiciech Frykowski, Abigail Folger, Steven Parent, and Jay Sebring are killed.

August 9, 1969
Leno and Rosemary LaBianca are killed.

September 30, 1969
Manson moves his followers to Barker Ranch in Death Valley, California.

October 12, 1969
Sheriffs raid Barker Ranch; Manson and twenty-one others are jailed for arson and auto theft.

December 1, 1969
Los Angeles police chief Edward Davis announces the case "solved."

December 2, 1969
Linda Kasabian surrenders to authorities in Concord, New Hampshire.

December 5, 1969
Atkins begins testimony before the grand jury.

December 8, 1969
Indictments are handed down against six Family members, including Manson.

December 12, 1969
Fingerprints found at murder scenes are matched to Tex Watson and Patricia Krenwinkel.

December 24, 1969
The judge rules that Manson may represent himself.

February 28, 1970
Kasabian is granted immunity in exchange for testimony.

March 6, 1970
Atkins meets with Manson, then fires her attorney; Manson is stripped of power to represent himself.

July 24, 1970
Testimony begins.

August 3, 1970
President Richard Nixon expresses the opinion that Manson is guilty.

October 5, 1970
Manson attacks Judge Charles Older.

November 16, 1970
The state rests.

November 19, 1970
The defense rests.

November 20, 1970
Manson gives a statement in court without the jury present.

November 30, 1970
Court resumes after a break; attorney Ron Hughes is missing.

January 15, 1971
The prosecution finishes its closing arguments; the jury starts deliberations.

January 25, 1971
All defendants are convicted on murder and conspiracy to commit murder.

March 29, 1971
The death penalty is given to all defendants.

February 18, 1972
The death penalty is stricken; the Tate-LaBianca killers have death sentences commuted to life imprisonment.

For Further Reading

Jess Bravin, *Squeaky: The Life and Times of Lynette Alice Fromme.* New York: St. Martin's, 1997. A well-researched and compelling look into one of the only remaining members of the Manson Family. A look at her "baby boomer" childhood through her attempted assassination of President Gerald Ford.

Edward George and Dary Matera, *Taming the Beast: Charles Manson's Life Behind Bars.* New York: St. Martin's, 1998. An account of Manson during his incarceration after the Tate murders by a prison counselor with insight into the day-to-day existence of the notorious inmate.

Greg King, *Sharon Tate and the Manson Murders.* New York: Barricade Books, 2000. A thoughtful and well-researched biography of actress Sharon Tate and the events and days leading up to her death.

Jay Robert Nash, *Bloodletters and Badmen.* New York: Evans, 1995. A look at two centuries of American criminals, with a long entry on Manson.

Works Consulted

Books

Susan Atkins, *Child of Satan, Child of God*. Plainfield, NJ: Logos International, 1977. The first-person account of Family member Susan "Sadie" Atkins, from her unhappy home life to her days with Manson and her religious conversion in prison.

Vincent Bugliosi, *Outrage*. New York: W.W. Norton, 1996. Bugliosi's extended essay on the injustice of the O.J. Simpson double-murder trial, with comparisons to the Manson trial.

Vincent Bugliosi with Curt Gentry, *Helter Skelter: The True Story of the Manson Murders*. Rev. ed., New York: W.W. Norton, 1994. A thorough account of the Manson trial as seen from the eyes of the prosecutor. Masterfully laid out by veteran writer Curt Gentry. The best-selling true crime book of all time.

Joan Didion, *The White Album*. New York: Simon and Schuster, 1979. A retrospective on the issues and personalities of the 1960s by the biographer of Linda Kasabian.

John Gilmore and Ron Kenner, *The Garbage People*. Los Angeles: Amok, 1995. A look into the lesser-known members of the Manson Family.

Thomas Kiernan, *The Roman Polanski Story*. New York: Grove, 1980. An unflattering look at the Oscar-winning, controversial film director, including his childhood in Poland during World War II, his glamorous life with Sharon Tate in Hollywood, and his life as a fugitive from justice.

David Leaf, *The Beach Boys*. Philadelphia: Courage Books, 1978. An account of the popular music group and the culture of Southern California during the 1960s, with a chapter on Manson's involvement with Beach Boys member Dennis Wilson.

Clara Livsey, *The Manson Women: A "Family" Portrait*. New York: Richard Marek, 1980. An examination of the collective psychology of Patricia Krenwinkel, Susan Atkins, and Leslie Van Houten.

Charles Manson and Nuel Emmons, *Charles Manson: In His Own Words*. New York: Grove, 1986. Manson cooperated with a former prison acquaintance in this first-person account of his life. Although insightful and colorful, the book's style fails to capture Manson's personality.

John Phillips with Jim Jerome, *Papa John*. New York: Doubleday, 1986. The autobiography of popular musician John Phillips, who was a neighbor of the Polanskis and was at one point a suspect in the murder of Sharon Tate.

Roman Polanski, *Roman*. New York: William Morrow, 1984. The unrepentant autobiography of the controversial film director.

Ed Sanders, *The Family*. New York: Dutton, 1971. Despite his newspaper's reputation as a radical underground newspaper, Sanders of the *Los Angeles Free Press* provided the most insightful and level-headed commentary during the Manson trial. This is his account of the Family and the trial.

Charles Watson, *Will You Die For Me?* Old Tappan, NJ: Revell, 1978. The convicted murderer tells of his years growing up in Texas, the nine months he spent with the Manson Family, the murders, and the religious rebirth he experienced in 1975 when he became a Christian.

Theo Wilson, *Headline Justice*. New York: Thunder's Mouth, 1996. This book offers anecdotal essays by an award-winning journalist on the three decades of criminal trials she covered as a reporter for the *New York Daily News*.

Periodicals

David Dalton and David Felton, "'Year of the Fork, Night of the Hunter.'" *Rolling Stone*, June 12, 1970.

Larry DuBois, "Interview—Roman Polanski," *Playboy*, December 1971.

Barry Ferrell, "In Hollywood, the Dead Keep Right on Dying," *Life*, November 14, 1969.

Karl Flemming, "The Manson Scene," *Newsweek*, January 4, 1971.

John Kendall, "Ball Reports to Judge," *Los Angeles Times*, December 25, 1969.

———, "Linda Kasabian Testifies She Loved Manson as the 'Messiah,'" *Los Angles Times*, August 6, 1970.

————, "Manson Asks for a 'Voice,'" *Los Angeles Times*, December 18, 1969.

————, "Manson Attacks Judge," *Los Angeles Times*, October 6, 1970.

————, "Manson Loses Pro Per," *Los Angeles Times*, March 6, 1970.

————, "Manson, Three Girls Receive Death Penalty," *Los Angeles Times*, March 30, 1971.

————, "Mrs. Kasabian's Testimony Met by 50 Defense Objections," *Los Angeles Times*, July 28, 1970, p. 20.

————, "Witness Begins Story," *Los Angeles Times*, July 27, 1970.

Los Angeles Free Press, "Manson's 'Nixon' Statement," August 10, 1970.

Los Angeles Free Press, "News in Brief: Manson's 'X' Statement," July 31–August 6, 1970.

Los Angeles Times, "Text of Nixon Remarks on Press and Manson," August 4, 1970.

Peter Maas, "The Sharon Tate Murder Case," *Ladies Home Journal*, April 1970.

Robert Newell, "Dream Comes True for Lad; He's Going to Boys Town," *Indianapolis News*, March 7, 1949.

Steven Roberts, "Charles Manson: One Man's Family," *New York Times Magazine*, January 4, 1970.

Lawrence Schiller, "Susan Atkins' Story of Two Nights of Murder," *Los Angeles Times*, December 14, 1969.

Time, "Hippies and Violence: The Demon of Death Valley," December 12, 1969.

Time, "Nothing But Bodies," August 15, 1969.

Video

CBS News/A&E Network, *The Twentieth Century*. Vol. 3. A&E Home Video, 1994, videocassette. Despite a few minor factual inaccuracies, this is a compact and well-produced visual documentary on the Manson trial, with clips and video of the cast of characters.

Internet Sources

The Manson Murders, (www.mansonmurders.com). This site offers information about the present-day whereabouts and activities of all associated with the Manson trial.

Findlaw, (www.findlaw.com). An invaluable resource, since most libraries do not have U.S. Supreme Court, U.S. District Court, or state supreme court decisions. Court decisions include every justice's opinion in its entirety with footnotes. Justices' references to other decisions are linked to those decisions.

Websites

Crime Library. (www. crimelibrary.com/manson/mansonmain.htm). A comprehensive website featuring in-depth looks at hundreds of criminal cases. The well-written article on Manson is indebted to Vincent Bugliosi's account, but it is a worthwhile synopsis.

State v. Charles Manson: Seminar in Famous Trials. (www.law. umkc.edu/faculty/projects/Ftrials/manson/manson.htm). A concise website devoted to the Manson case. Very derivative of Vincent Bugliosi's book, but useful as an overview.

Index

Picture Credits

About the Authors

Bradley Steffens is the author of twenty-two nonfiction books for
young adults, including *Furman v. Georgia*, *Censorship*, and *Free
Speech*. He lives in Escondido, California, with his wife, Angela.

Craig L. Staples grew up in Dallas, Texas, where he attended St.
Thomas Aquinas School. He graduated from Duke University in
1979. He makes his home in Oklahoma City.